To

....

From

....

Date

....

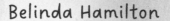

Belinda Hamilton

Good Night, GOD

Bedtime Prayers for Girls

BARBOUR **kidz**
A Division of Barbour Publishing

Published by Barbour Publishing, Inc., 1810 Barbour Drive, Uhrichsville, Ohio 44683, www.barbourbooks.com

Our mission is to inspire the world with the life-changing message of the Bible.

Member of the
Evangelical Christian
Publishers Association

Printed in China.

001303 0822 HA

Did you know that you can talk to God about anything? It's true!

If you're not sure how to talk to Him, you can begin with the bedtime prayers in this book. The prayers here cover topics like

- love
- courage
- worries
- friendship
- kindness
- and so much more!

Spending time talking with God before bed each night is the very best way to end your day. Just try it and see for yourself!

You're Forgiven

You must be kind to each other. Think
of the other person. Forgive other
people just as God forgave you.
EPHESIANS 4:32

God, friends sometimes hurt my feelings. Then I get sad and maybe even a little angry. I don't know what to do. I need Your help to get rid of the bad feelings in my heart.

It's so hard to forgive my friends when they do or say hurtful things. But I know You want me to show Your love by being a forgiving person, Lord. You always forgive me when I make mistakes—even when I've done something terrible. And You still love me, no matter what! You are such a good God!

Today, help me to say, "I forgive you." If You can erase my mistakes from Your mind, I can do the same for my friends. Thank You, God, and good night!

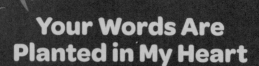

Your Words Are Planted in My Heart

"But those which fell on good ground
have heard the Word. They keep it
in a good and true heart and they
keep on giving good grain."
LUKE 8:15

It is so cool to know, God, that Your Word can grow inside me. It's like planting a flower seed in good soil. I need to make sure to give it plenty of water and put it where the sun can shine on it. Soon, with care, little sprouts will pop up. Before long, a beautiful flower stands tall and strong, giving beauty to the world around it.

That's how I want to be, God. I want Your rich Word planted deep within my heart. Then it can be watered with Your truth and washed in the dazzling light of Your love. Help me to grow strong and un-shakable so I can show off the beauty of Your love to the world.

Thank You for the Bible. It is full of all the good ingredients I need to grow up to be the kind of girl You want me to be. Good night, God.

Sing a New Song

He put a new song in my mouth, a song
of praise to our God. Many will see and
fear and will put their trust in the Lord.

PSALM 40:3

God, I am thankful that You made music. When I
am glad, I sing. Sharing the music inside me makes
me happy. It's a good way for me to show my joy.

But sometimes, when I'm unhappy, it's hard to
hear the music inside me. I know those unhappy
feelings won't last forever, but sometimes it's just hard
to get past hard feelings. I don't like those feelings,
and I know You don't want me to feel that way either.

I know You are always close by to whisper a new
song in my heart and bring back my joy. Help me
to let go of my hurt feelings and listen for Your new
song. Thank You, God, and good night!

God's Plan for Me

"'For I know the plans I have for you,' says the Lord, 'plans for well-being and not for trouble, to give you a future and a hope.'"
JEREMIAH 29:11

God, I'm so glad that You made a plan for my whole life. Before You made the heavens, the sky, and the earth, You thought about me and planned everything for me. Now, when I put my future in Your hands, I don't have to worry or be afraid about growing older.

I know I sometimes need to be reminded that it's You I belong to. And because I am Yours, I need to be kind and considerate to others. But You are always quick to forgive me when I ask.

Thank You for giving me a future of hope that means I will always be part of Your plan. Good night, God.

Don't Be Afraid

"Do not fear, for I am with you. Do not be afraid, for I am your God. I will give you strength, and for sure I will help you. Yes, I will hold you up with My right hand that is right and good."

ISAIAH 41:10

God, I try to be strong, but sometimes I'm afraid. Sometimes I don't even know why I'm scared—I just am. I don't like the way I feel when I'm afraid.

I'm glad that Your Word says that because You are my God, I don't have to be afraid. Knowing You are always with me makes me feel safe.

Help me to remember when I get scared that You are right there with me. You hold me up and protect me and even make me strong. Thank You for letting me know that You never leave me alone. Good night, God.

Be a Good Friend

"Do for other people whatever you
would like to have them do for
you. This is what the Jewish Law
and the early preachers said."

MATTHEW 7:12

God, sometimes I get upset when I don't get to do things my way. When that happens, I don't always treat my friends or family the way I should.

I know I'm supposed to treat my friends the way I want to be treated. But sometimes that's hard when it's something I really want to do. It makes me sad when I treat a friend badly. I know I should apologize.

With Your forgiveness and help, I can say I'm sorry and learn to be a better friend. Thank You for being forgiving. Help me to be a good friend and family member and to treat others the way I want to be treated. Good night, God.

The Rainbow, God's Sign of Love

"When I bring clouds over the earth
and the rain-bow is seen in the clouds,
I will remember My agreement that is
between Me and you and every living thing
of all flesh. Never again will the water
become a flood to destroy all flesh."

GENESIS 9:14–15

I love Your rainbow, God! I love to draw and color pictures of Your rainbow. It reminds me that You always keep Your promises. It also reminds me that You are looking down and thinking about me and every living thing. And that You love the world You created.

A rainbow has all the beautiful colors that are in my crayon box. That shows me that You use all the colors to create. You are an awesome God to make such an awesome sign to show us we can trust whatever You say.

Thank You for Your promises. And thank You for Your rainbow for the world to see, and know, that You are God. Good night.

Your Amazing Creatures

O Lord, how many are Your works! You made them all in wisdom. The earth is full of what You have made. There is the wide sea full of both large and small animals. There are too many for us to number.

PSALM 104:24–25

God, I laugh when I think about all the funny-looking animals You created. I wonder if they make You laugh too. Especially porcupines with their pointy quills and narwhals that look like they swam right out of a mystical book. I like the funny way crabs walk and the super-slow way sloths move. You were so creative to make bouncy kangaroos, long-necked ostriches, and humongous whales.

Thank You, God, for giving us so many interesting, strange-looking, and amazing creatures to look at and enjoy. Good night.

Don't Pretend to Be Something You're Not

"How can you say to your brother, 'Let me take that small piece of wood out of your eye,' when there is a big piece of wood in your own eye? You who pretend to be someone you are not, first take the big piece of wood out of your own eye. Then you can see better to take the small piece of wood out of your brother's eye."

MATTHEW 7:4–5

God, there are times when I pretend I'm perfect when I know I'm not. Sometimes I even point out things my friends have done, even though I have done something just as bad or worse.

It's really hard to admit when I have done something wrong. But when I do, I feel better afterward because I know it's what You want me to do.

Thank You for forgiving me when I admit the things that I have done wrong in Your eyes. Help me to remember that I'm not perfect. That Your Son, Jesus, is the only perfect person to ever live. Help me to be more like Jesus. Good night, God.

Because God Cares

"Look at the birds in the sky. They do not plant seeds. They do not gather grain. They do not put grain into a building to keep. Yet your Father in heaven feeds them! Are you not more important than the birds?"

MATTHEW 6:26

I see how much You care for the birds in the sky, the animals in the woods, and the fish in the sea, God. They don't have grocery stores, kitchens, or refrigerators to store food, yet they never go hungry. Birds don't plant the seeds that grow the grain. Neither do bees plant the flower seeds they make honey from. But You make sure they have food to eat.

And You love people a lot more than birds or bees, fish or other animals. And because I know that You care for the tiniest living things, I won't worry. I can trust that You will always care for me and my family.

Thank You, God, that You provide food for birds and bees—all Your creatures—and me. Good night.

Do Good and Be Happy

Be happy in the Lord. And He will
give you the desires of your heart.
Give your way over to the Lord. Trust
in Him also. And He will do it.
PSALM 37:4–5

God, You give me choices every day. Sometimes I wish for things and don't even ask You if You want me to have them. I even want things I don't need or shouldn't have. There are times when what I'm wanting doesn't even make sense. It just sounds good at the moment.

I want the good things You have planned for me to be the things that make me happy. Those are the things that will make good sense in the end.

Help me to have the same wants and wishes You have for me. That way I will grow up and be happy. I trust You, God. Thanks, and good night, God.

When Things Seem Too Big

I can do all things because
Christ gives me the strength.
PHILIPPIANS 4:13

When things seem too big or too hard, it's easy to want to give up. It can be scary when someone asks me to do something that I'm not good at or have never done before.

But God, You are always with me and ready to stand beside me when I need help. And because You are with me, I can do whatever it is You want me to do. You are able to give me all the strength and courage I need to do what is good and right in Your sight. When something seems too big for me, I can ask for Your help.

Remind me that You are always here with me to help me and guide me. And thank You, God, for giving me the strength and courage to do whatever You ask me to do. Good night, God.

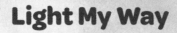

Light My Way

Your Word is a lamp to my
feet and a light to my path.
PSALM 119:105

The Bible says Your Word is like a lamp for my feet.
This means that the Bible can shine light on the way
I'm supposed to live. I don't have to walk in the dark.
And I won't be alone because You will be with me.

Just as it is hard to find my way around a dark
room without a flashlight, it is hard to find my way
in life without the light of Your Word. I could bump
into all kinds of obstacles and trip and fall and hurt
myself. Life without Your Word would be scary.

But the Bible tells me how to act no matter what
I'm doing. God, thank You for not leaving me in the
dark and for lighting the way for me wherever I go.
Good night.

I Am Saved

"For God so loved the world that He gave His only Son. Whoever puts his trust in God's Son will not be lost but will have life that lasts forever."

JOHN 3:16

God, I understand that Adam and Eve were the first people You created. And they disobeyed You. This put the curse of sin on everyone in the world. It put a divide between all humans and You, God.

But, because You loved people so much, You sent Your only Son to save us. Jesus had to die to save me, my family, and my friends from the awful curse of sin. The only way Jesus could do that was because He is perfect, just like You. And because Jesus is God, He defeated sin. Death and the grave could not hold Him.

Thank You, God, for sending Your Son to save me. Good night!

The Best Gift Ever

Our hope comes from God. May He
fill you with joy and peace because of
your trust in Him. May your hope grow
stronger by the power of the Holy Spirit.
ROMANS 15:13

Because I am Yours, God, I don't have to worry about what will happen to me when I die. I will be with You and Jesus forever and ever. Jesus made that possible. Heaven will be awesome.

I want to give all my friends the gifts of joy and peace that come from belonging to Jesus. Those are the best gifts I could ever give anyone. Jesus is the best gift I ever received. Help me to share You with everyone.

You are a God of hope. And Your gift is the Holy Spirit for everyone who believes. Thank You for the best gift ever. I love You. Good night, God.

Be a Good Friend

So comfort each other and make each
other strong as you are already doing.
1 THESSALONIANS 5:11

Thank You, God, that You give me friends to share my life with. Friends who make me feel better when I am sad or not feeling well. Friends who celebrate happy times with me too. Good friends can really add a lot to my life. But first I have to be a good friend.

Help me to be the kind of friend I want and need. I want to help my friends to feel better when they are sad by listening to them. And when they are sick, I want to remember them in my prayers and let them know I miss them.

Help me not to be shy about making new friends, because to have a friend, I need to be a friend. Good night, God.

Listen to Others

He who is careful in what he says has
much learning, and he who has a quiet
spirit is a man of understanding.
PROVERBS 17:27

God, it's hard to watch what I say. It feels as if words
are able to leap right out of my mouth sometimes.
Words leave my mouth before I have time to think
about whether I should say them out loud.

And sometimes when someone is trying to talk
to me, I find it hard to be still and quietly listen. Sitting and listening can make me wiggly and uncom-
fortable. Often my mind wanders and I don't hear
what is being said to me.

Help me to put a lock on my mouth so that I
won't say hurtful or disrespectful things. God, if You
help me to be still and listen quietly, I won't get into
trouble. You are a good Helper, God. Thank You,
and good night!

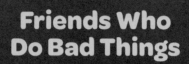

Friends Who Do Bad Things

Do not let anyone fool you. Bad people can make those who want to live good become bad.

1 CORINTHIANS 15:33

God, I know some kids who do and say things they shouldn't. It's hard not to want to fit in. It seems easier just to go along with what others are doing, even if I know it's wrong. I don't want to be left out or be made fun of.

I know the bad stuff kids do is going to hurt them someday. Because You love people, You won't let us get away with doing bad things forever. I don't want You to have to discipline me. So please help me listen to Your voice and stay away from people who do bad things. Don't let me be fooled into thinking bad behavior is okay, because I know it's not. I want to be friends with other kids who love You. Thank You, God, and good night.

God's Gifts

God has given each of you a gift.
Use it to help each other. This
will show God's loving-favor.
1 PETER 4:10

I am so excited to know that You give Your children gifts, God. Not gifts like toys that we get tired of and throw away. You give gifts that can be used to celebrate and share You with others.

I may not know for sure what my gift is yet. But I know that if I ask, You will eventually show me when the time is right. It may be that I will have the gift of music or writing, speaking or teaching. Maybe I will be gifted to counsel others who are struggling or need to be listened to.

Whatever it is, God, I know You will show me how to use these wonderful and powerful God-given gifts. Thank You for the gifts You give. Good night.

A Forever Crown

Everyone who runs in a race does many
things so his body will be strong. He
does it to get a crown that will soon
be worth nothing, but we work for
a crown that will last forever.

1 CORINTHIANS 9:25

Crowns are beautiful, God. Often they are given to someone who has done something really well. A person works really hard to win a race. But soon someone beats that person, and the crown is theirs for a while. Those kinds of crowns don't last.

But the crowns You give for winning Your race are different. Your race is about sharing the good news of Jesus with others. They are the most beautiful crowns ever. And they never rust. They last forever and ever.

That's the kind of crown I want, God. It means You are proud of me for working hard to tell others about Your Son and all He has done for us. Thank You, God, for Your dazzling crowns that last forever.

Good night, God.

Perfectly Planned for Me

There are many plans in a man's heart,
but it is the Lord's plan that will stand.
PROVERBS 19:21

God, I make lots of plans. They don't always turn out the way I want. In fact, sometimes they turn out to be something I wish I had never done. I don't know why things don't always turn out the way I dreamed or hoped they would. But Your Word says that Your plans turn out perfectly. Please help me to remember to talk to You about the plans my heart makes. That way I won't worry about how they will turn out. You make sure all Your plans work out the best way possible.

I am grateful that You will listen to me about my plans and lead me in the right direction. Thank You, and good night, God.

Feeling Guilty

"For God did not send His Son into the
world to say it is guilty. He sent His
Son so the world might be saved from
the punishment of sin by Him."
JOHN 3:17

God, I don't like it when someone points out that I
did something wrong. Feeling guilty is a bad feeling.
When I disobey or hurt someone's feelings, I feel really
guilty afterward. I know that feeling is You telling me
that I need to say I'm sorry. And then not do it again.

You don't point out my sins to make me feel bad.
You do it because You love me. You know my sin will
lead me down roads that will cause pain and trouble
later. I don't want to go down those roads. I want
to be forgiven by You and stay close by Your side.

Thank You for pointing out the things I do wrong
and helping me to quickly say I'm sorry. That is the
way to live a happy life. Good night, God.

Don't Be Wishy-Washy

Jesus Christ is the same yesterday
and today and forever.
HEBREWS 13:8

God, I change my mind a lot. I think I know what I want to wear or what game to play or what snack to eat but then change my mind. It makes a mess of my room. And that can make my parents upset with me. I wish I could just make a choice and stick with it. But my mind is wishy-washy.

Your mind never changes, God. Every choice You've made and everything You've ever said stays exactly the same. You're perfect, so every decision You make is perfect.

I like that You don't change Your mind. That means You will never change Your mind about loving me. Thank You for not being wishy-washy, God. Good night.

Show Me

Someone may say, "You have faith, and
I do things. Prove to me you have faith
when you are doing nothing. I will prove
to you I have faith by doing things."

JAMES 2:18

God, I know that I'm not saved by the things I do. But
I do good things to show other people that I belong
to You and want to serve You. All my good works
will never make me perfect, because perfection is a
yardstick that I can never measure up to. That's why
Jesus came down—so You could see Jesus' perfection
in me. Still, doing good and sharing You is a sign that
Jesus lives in my heart and that I believe His words.

Your Spirit in me helps me remember to be kind
and helpful to others. By living like Jesus, I can show
everyone that Jesus is real and living inside me. Thank
You, and good night, God.

Do My Best

So if you eat or drink or whatever
you do, do everything to honor God.
1 CORINTHIANS 10:31

Because I belong to You, God, I want to do everything my very best, whether it's schoolwork or helping my parents at home. I even want to eat healthy foods like I'm told so I can grow up strong and have lots of energy—even if I'd rather eat junk food. I want everything I do to honor You. And I know that's what You want for me too.

When I do my best, it reminds me that I belong to You and that You are able to use everything good I do to help with Your plans. The best part is that others can see that I am Yours when I do my best work.

Help me always to do the kind of work that will make You proud of me. Thank You, God. Good night.

One of a Kind

For You made the parts inside me. You put me together inside my mother. I will give thanks to You, for the greatness of the way I was made brings fear. Your works are great and my soul knows it very well.
PSALM 139:13–14

God, sometimes I'm not happy with the way I look. At times I wish I looked like someone else. But You took the time to make me different from everyone else in the world. No one else is exactly like me. I am unique.

I am remarkably and wonderfully created. No two stars in the heavens are alike. You created each star unique and special, just as You created me. I am special in Your eyes because there is no one exactly like me.

It's hard for me to imagine how difficult it must have been to come up with so many one-of-a-kinds. Thank You, God, that I am wonderfully created and one of a kind. Good night!

God-Sized Love

We have come to know and believe
the love God has for us. God is
love. If you live in love, you live by
the help of God and God lives in you.
1 JOHN 4:16

God, I use the word *love* all the time. I love clothes and dressing up, playing games with friends, bouncing up and down on the bed, and all kinds of foods. But there's a different and better kind of love. It's the kind of love that comes only from You. It's the kind of love that gives everything You have, including what You love the most.

That's the kind of love You have for me, God. You love me so much that You gave what You loved the most: Your only Son to come save me. In fact, everything You do is always from the biggest place of love ever. You *are* love, God.

Help me to see that there's a big difference between really liking stuff and God-sized love. Thank You for loving me, God, and good night.

Kindness

A woman who was a follower lived
in the city of Joppa. Her name was
Tabitha, or Dorcas. She did many good
things and many acts of kindness.

ACTS 9:36

God, I want to be known as a kind person like Dorcas. But sometimes it's hard when someone is mean to me. I know I shouldn't try to get even when someone does or says something bad to me. Even if someone is unkind to me, I want to show them kindness.

Your Word says that Dorcas was a follower. She did "many" good things and "many" acts of kindness. To have done so many good things, she must have always been thinking about others. That's how I want to be—thinking less about myself and more about doing kind, thoughtful things for others.

I'm happy to know that You thought enough of Dorcas, who showed so much kindness, to tell us about her. Thank You, God, and good night.

Don't Sink

Jesus said, "Come!" Peter got out of the
boat and walked on the water to Jesus.
But when he saw the strong wind, he was
afraid. He began to go down in the water.
He cried out, "Lord, save me!" At once
Jesus put out His hand and took hold
of him. Jesus said to Peter, "You have
so little faith! Why did you doubt?"
MATTHEW 14:29–31

Who wouldn't be afraid to do what Peter did, God?
He got out of a boat when the waves were big and
splashing all around. That's how doing new things
can be—*scary*—even if I know I'm doing them for a
good reason.

But just as You were there with Peter, You will be
with me. Your hand will reach out to keep me from
sinking. With You there's no reason to be afraid to
get out of the boat.

Help me to look for You and keep my eyes on You,
God. For as long as I keep my eyes on You, I won't
have to fear sinking. Thanks, and good night, God.

Christmas Gifts

The angel said to them, "Do not be afraid.
See! I bring you good news of great joy
which is for all people. Today, One Who saves
from the punishment of sin has been born
in the city of David. He is Christ the Lord."
LUKE 2:10–11

Even when it's not wintertime, I like to think about Christmas. It's my favorite time of the year. I love decorating the tree and singing songs, getting presents and decorating cookies. There's nothing like it. It makes me feel warm inside toward others.

But the greatest reason Christmas is so special, God, is because You gave us the best gift ever. You gave us a reason to celebrate every moment of every day of the year. You gave the world the gift of Jesus—not tied up with a bow but wrapped in swaddling clothes. And because He came to the world as a baby who had to learn to walk and talk, I know that Jesus understands everything about me.

Thank You for loving me and for the Christmas gift that came wrapped in swaddling clothes. Good night, God.

Bright Light

Jesus spoke to all the people, saying,
"I am the Light of the world. Anyone who
follows Me will not walk in darkness.
He will have the Light of Life."
JOHN 8:12

God, I don't like walking around in the dark. Not seeing where I'm going is scary. It's easy to bump into things. So it's good to have a light when it's dark.

I'm glad You're the "Light of the world." You shine Your light on other kinds of darkness in the world too. Things like bad choices and treating others badly. If I follow You and obey, I won't make bad choices or be mean to others, because Your light will shine on the bad things and help me to make better decisions.

It's good to know that You are full of light, and because You live within me, I won't have to walk alone in dark places. Thank You, God. Good night.

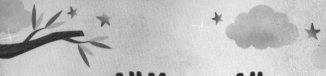

All Means *All*

Jesus said to him, "'You must love the Lord
your God with all your heart and with all
your soul and with all your mind.' This
is the first and greatest of the Laws."
MATTHEW 22:37–38

God, *all* is an important word. Especially when You
say it. All means everything of something. Not just a
little bit or even half of it. All means *all*.

You want every part of me to show that I love
You. That means my mind and heart, my arms and
legs, my ears and mouth—every part of me should
show my love for You.

I love You, God. Loving You is the most important thing in my life. Without You I wouldn't even
exist. I owe You everything. I can show how much
I love You by the things I do and the things I say or
listen to. I want all I do to come from a place of love
for You. Good night.

Obeying My Parents

Children, obey your parents in everything.
The Lord is pleased when you do.

COLOSSIANS 3:20

God, forgive me when I disobey my parents or when I'm disrespectful to them. I know it makes You sad for me to act that way. When I do, it's the same thing as disobeying or disrespecting You.

You put my parents and other adults over me to guide me and help me grow up making good decisions. Their job is to correct and lead me. My job is to listen and obey.

God, I want to please You by obeying and being respectful to my parents, my teachers, and other adults. Help me to ask for forgiveness when I don't act the way You want me to. Thank You, God. Good night.

Swallowed Up Whole

Then Jonah prayed to the Lord his
God while in the stomach of the fish,
saying, "I called out to the Lord because
of my trouble, and He answered me. I
cried for help from the place of the
dead, and You heard my voice."

JONAH 2:1–2

God, Jonah tried to run away from You. You told
Jonah to go warn some people—people he didn't
like. He was to tell them that You could see all the
evil things they were doing and that You were not
happy with them. You wanted Jonah to go because
You cared about the people, and You wanted to
save them. But because Jonah didn't like them, he
disobeyed and ran away. He didn't get far before
a big fish swallowed him up—whole.

I wouldn't like to be swallowed up by a big fish. I
want to obey You, even if that means doing something
I don't want to do. You see everything, God.

Help me to care enough about others so that
when You send me to tell them something, I'll go.
That way I can be a part of saving them, and You'll
be happy with me. Good night, God.

Signs

Give thanks to Him Who made the great
lights, for His loving-kindness lasts forever.
He made the sun to rule during the day,
for His loving-kindness lasts forever. He
made the moon and stars to rule during the
night, for His loving-kindness lasts forever.

PSALM 136:7–9

God, I am amazed when I think that You created
everything. You made the sun that shines bright
during the day. You made the moon and stars to
glow at night. You made rain to water the plants.
And You created forests, oceans, and jungles for all
kinds of animals to live in.

The reason You created this big, beautiful world
is because You love people—*all* the people of the
world. There's never been a person You didn't create
and love and care for. Even the air was made for
our lungs to breathe. You created more things for
us than I can even think about!

Thank You, God, for Your love that lasts forever.
Good night.

Like Sheep

"The one who watches the door opens it
for him. The sheep listen to the voice
of the shepherd. He calls his own sheep
by name and he leads them out. When
the shepherd walks ahead of them, they
follow him because they know his voice."

JOHN 10:3–4

God, You are the Good Shepherd. Those who follow
You are Your flock. We are like sheep. To be safe, we
need someone who is stronger and wiser and who
cares for us to lead us. Sheep can be pretty dumb
at times. They wander off and get lost.

I can be like that too. I wander away from You
and then realize that I have lost my way. That's why
I constantly have to listen for the voice of Your Holy
Spirit and read my Bible. Those are the ways You
guide me.

I am glad that I have a Good Shepherd to listen
to and follow after. Thank You, God, for leading me
and keeping me safe. Good night.

My BFF

Give all your worries to Him
because He cares for you.
1 PETER 5:7

You are my BFF, my best friend forever, God. No one cares or understands me like You do. Not even my best earthly friend. There are some things I don't want to talk to my friends about. Things that only You will understand. With You there's no judgment when I tell You what's bothering me.

You don't want me to carry my worries alone. And since You already know what I'm thinking, it won't be shocking news to You. And the best thing is that when I tell You what's on my mind, I can let it go and not worry about it anymore.

I'm so thankful to have You as my BFF. Good night, God.

Sweet as Honey

Pleasing words are like honey. They are sweet to the soul and healing to the bones.
PROVERBS 16:24

I like the taste of honey. It's sweet and sticks to my tongue and leaves a very pleasant taste in my mouth. But God, sometimes my words leave a bad taste in my mouth. Right after I've said something rude, I wish I could take back my words.

Speaking can be like listening to a pretty song. If someone hits an off-key note, it can ruin the song. It's not a very pleasant sound to those who hear it.

I want to speak sweet words like honey. I don't want my words to taste or sound sour. Help me to hold back the sour notes and say words that are as sweet and yummy as honey. Thank You, and good night, God.

Wings like Eagles

But they who wait upon the Lord will get new strength. They will rise up with wings like eagles. They will run and not get tired. They will walk and not become weak.

ISAIAH 40:31

Sometimes I get tired, God. Tired of school and homework or of chores at home. Sometimes I have so much to do that I just want to give up and quit.

It would be nice to have wings like an eagle and just glide on the air. To soar and never get tired or weak. When I spend time with You, I get that feeling. You give me the strength and energy I need to help me finish what I start. You can even make me excited to do something that seems boring or tiring.

Thank You for being with me when I'm tired. I know that feeling won't last forever. It won't be long before I'm up and running strong again. Good night, God.

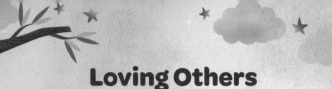

Loving Others

"The second is like it, 'You must love your neighbor as you love yourself.'"
MATTHEW 22:39

Your first command for me is to love You with all my heart. The second is to love others as much as I love myself. That could take some practice. I usually think of myself and what I want a whole lot more than I do others. It may mean spending time to do a good deed instead of playing. Or it may mean letting someone go ahead of me in line or letting them have the last piece of cake.

Forgive me, God, for not loving others more. Help me to learn that I'm not more important than anyone else.

Because You loved me and put me first, I want to put others before myself. Thank You, God. Good night.

Daniel's God

"My God sent His angel and shut the lions'
mouths. They have not hurt me, because He
knows that I am not guilty, and because
I have done nothing wrong to you, O king."
Then the king was very pleased and had
Daniel taken up out of the hole in the
ground. So they took Daniel out of the
hole and saw that he had not been hurt
at all, because he had trusted in his God.

DANIEL 6:22–23

The morning after Daniel had been thrown into the
den of hungry lions, King Darius ran to see if You,
Daniel's God, had saved him. He was happy to see
Daniel alive, standing tall and well. It was proof that
You are the one true God.

I know that You can shut the mouths of hungry
lions. You have charge over everything in heaven
and on earth. You are the only One who can bring
people out of danger and save them. That's because
You are the living God, and You will rule forever.

Thank You, God, for stories that tell us of Your
great power. Good night, God.

Lions and Bears, Oh My!

And David said, "The Lord Who saved me from the foot of the lion and from the foot of the bear, will save me from the hand of this Philistine." Saul said to David, "Go, and may the Lord be with you."

1 SAMUEL 17:37

Lions and bears are scary. David was a young shepherd boy, and already he had fought scary animals. He had a job to do. That job was to watch over his family's sheep in the field and keep them safe. He wasn't afraid because he knew God was with him.

Sometimes I face scary things. Not lions or bears, but things that are scary to me. And because I know that You helped David do courageous things as a boy, I trust that You will help me. Things that seem impossible to me aren't impossible for You, God. Thank You for helping boys and girls do scary and hard things. Good night, God!

Grumpy Pants

He who is slow to anger is better than
the powerful. And he who rules his spirit
is better than he who takes a city.

PROVERBS 16:32

Sometimes I wear grumpy pants. It's not that I'm mad at anybody. My face just forgets to be happy. Sometimes I wake up that way. Mostly it's when I'm tired or hungry. I'm probably hard to be around when I have on my grumpy pants.

God, help me to know when my face isn't happy. And show me how to quickly turn my frown into a smile. Help me to be pleasant to be around. It may mean that I need to feed my hungry tummy or take a break and rest. But it could mean that I need to turn everything off at night and go to bed earlier to get a good sleep. That way I can start the day rested and not wearing grumpy pants.

Thank You, God, that You are never grumpy and for helping me not to be either. Good night, God.

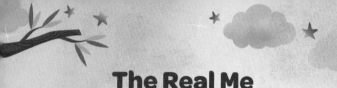

The Real Me

Do not act like the sinful people of the
world. Let God change your life. First
of all, let Him give you a new mind.
Then you will know what God wants
you to do. And the things you do will
be good and pleasing and perfect.
ROMANS 12:2

God, sometimes I think I want to be like someone
else. There are girls who are cuter, smarter, more
talented, and funnier than me. I could dress like them
or even try acting like them. But I don't think I would
feel like the real me.

I know You made me to be exactly who I am. I
want to be happy with the real me. Your Spirit is at
work inside me, making me exactly who You created
me to be. I don't want to think about what I'm not. I'd
rather think about what I am and can be.

Help me to remember that I am Yours and that
You are not finished working on me. Thank You that
I don't have to be like someone else. I can be exactly
how You made me because You love me just as I am.
Good night, God.

Not Funny

Do not be guilty of telling bad stories and of foolish talk. These things are not for you to do. Instead, you are to give thanks for what God has done for you.

EPHESIANS 5:4

Sometimes kids say or do "funny" things that I know I shouldn't laugh at. Especially if they are picking on someone. God, help me to see things the way You see them and not to laugh when something is rude or naughty. You gave me laughter to express my joy out loud. But I should feel no joy at something that is rude, or insults or hurts others. If I were in their place, I wouldn't want someone to laugh at me.

Thanks, God, for joy and for laughter. And thanks for helping me not to laugh at the wrong things. Good night, God.

Stuck

*If you are angry, do not let
it become sin. Get over your
anger before the day is finished.*

EPHESIANS 4:26

God, sometimes my mind gets stuck in an angry place, and I have a hard time getting unstuck. It can be confusing because part of me wants to get out of the angry place and part of me is happy to stay angry. Sometimes I'm waiting for someone to come and say, "I'm sorry." Or maybe I'm the one who needs to say, "I'm sorry." And then there are times when it's just about me waiting to get my way. I know that's not right.

Forgive me, God, when I stay angry all day. If I don't let the anger go, it could still be there when I wake up the next day. Being angry is not the way to end or start a day.

Help me to get out of my angry place as soon as I can. Help me to let go of things that have upset me and be willing to talk to someone about them calmly, without crying. Help me to see others' points of view, especially my parents'. Help me to leave my angry place. Thanks, and good night, God.

Still, Small Voice

After the earth shook, a fire came. But the Lord was not in the fire. And after the fire came a sound of gentle blowing.

1 KINGS 19:12

God, sometimes I get so busy I forget to listen for You. Maybe I'm waiting for You to yell at me to get my attention, like my parents or teachers sometimes have to do. But because You mostly choose to whisper, it is hard to hear You through all the noise. When You speak, I know that what You have to say is going to be very important. You need me to really listen. You want my full attention.

Help me, God, to turn down the noise and find a quiet place so I can hear Your whisper, which is like a gentle blowing. I don't want to miss a word of what You want to tell me.

Thank You, God, for getting my full attention and whispering great and wonderful things. Good night.

The Little Things

"He that is faithful with little things
is faithful with big things also. He
that is not honest with little things
is not honest with big things."

LUKE 16:10

Sometimes I forget to be happy about the little things in my life. Instead, I'm often thinking about the next big thing coming up. I'm either looking forward to or dreading what's coming up next. Dreading something, like a test or a doctor's appointment, can be upsetting. Having to wait for something that I'm looking forward to can make me fidgety. So concentrating on little things can be hard.

With time, everything passes—the fun stuff and the bad stuff. I wonder how many little things I've missed because I'm waiting for only the big things to happen. It's like looking at a flower garden and missing a tiny toad under a leaf or a bee in a blossom. I bet there are lots of cool little things I'm missing.

Help me, God, to enjoy all the little moments I might be missing. And help me to see all the wonderful little things, like toads and bees. Good night, God.

STOP!!!

A wise man fears God and turns
away from what is sinful, but a fool
is full of pride and is not careful.

PROVERBS 14:16

God, sometimes there are things ahead of us that
are dangerous. We have traffic signs that tell us to
stop and look for traffic. They are there to protect
drivers, their passengers, and pedestrians. Drivers
have to watch for them and be ready to stop.

You put signs in my path to protect me too, God.
Like traffic signs, Your signs help me to know when
to stop and think about what's happening at that
moment. They tell me I need to slow down and look
at things that are coming my way. Or maybe I need
to stop, turn around, and go in another direction. Your
signs are ways of warning me that danger lies ahead.

Thank You, God, for putting signs along the way
for me. I trust You because only You know what lies
ahead in my path. Good night.

Hugs

"This is what I tell you to do: Love each other just as I have loved you."
JOHN 15:12

God, sometimes I just need a hug. It doesn't mean that something's wrong. Maybe it's just that I need to feel safe and warm or feel loved at that moment. I think a lot of people need that.

You give hugs too, God. It's usually through other people. You put a feeling in someone's heart to hug a person. There are times when I have the feeling that I'm the one who is supposed to give a person a hug. Maybe they need to know that they're not alone.

Help me not to be shy when I have the feeling that I need to hug someone. Or at least give them a smile or ask, "How are you?" Thank You for Your hugs that You give through others. Good night, God.

The Trickster Gets Tricked

When the morning came, Jacob saw that it was Leah. He said to Laban, "What have you done to me? Did I not work for you for Rachel? Why have you fooled me?"

GENESIS 29:25

God, there are people in the Bible who played tricks on each other. Tricks that changed their lives. Jacob played a trick on his twin brother, Esau. Then years later Jacob himself was tricked by Laban. Jacob wanted to marry Rachel, and so he worked for her father, Laban, for seven years. After the seven years were up, Laban put his older daughter, Leah, in Rachel's place. Jacob, the trickster, had been tricked. He had to work for Laban another seven years to marry Rachel, the girl he loved.

I don't want to be a trickster or be tricked, God. I want to do all things honestly. That way I will feel good about myself.

Thank You, God, that You never trick anyone and that You can help me not to be tricked. Good night.

Ears Turned On

A fool does not find joy in understanding,
but only in letting his own mind be known.
PROVERBS 18:2

Everyone is different, God. Everyone has different opinions. But that's okay. We don't all have to think the same. That doesn't mean that I'm wrong about everything, but it sure doesn't mean that I'm always right about everything either. I need to be willing to listen to what others have to say. It's good to listen to others and hear their thoughts. I might find that what they are saying makes really good sense.

God, You might even be trying to teach me something through someone else. Help me to have my ears turned on. Help me not to be angry if someone disagrees with me. Show me ways that I can help someone else see my way when I think I'm right, without being rude about it.

I know the only one I cannot disagree with is You, God. Thank You for not letting me stay stuck when I'm wrong. You gave me ears to hear others. Good night, God.

Teach Me

Bring up a child by teaching him the
way he should go, and when he is old
he will not turn away from it.

PROVERBS 22:6

Thank You, God, for giving me parents and others
who teach me about You. They are a gift from You.
I want to let them know how thankful I am for them
taking the time and loving me enough to teach me
about You. Thank You for those who are showing
me, by example, how to be more like Jesus. Help me
to listen when they correct me when I'm not following what the Bible is teaching me.

Because I am being taught how to walk with
You while I'm young, God, my life will be easier
and better.

Help me to always remember to be thankful
for what I am learning about You. And help me to
always remember to thank the ones teaching me.
Good night, God.

My Face in the Mirror

Anyone who hears the Word of God and does not obey is like a man looking at his face in a mirror. After he sees himself and goes away, he forgets what he looks like.
JAMES 1:23–24

I like to look at myself in the mirror. I wonder what I will look like when I grow up. But You have a mirror for me to look at so I can see what I look like on the inside, God. It's the Bible. It tells me how I should look—not my face or my clothes, but messy stuff on the inside.

You want me to be kind and gentle, forgiving and caring for others. Those are the things that You think are beautiful. I want to be beautiful on the inside. I want Your love to shine from the inside out.

Thank You, God, for the Bible that tells me what I need to change in order to be beautiful on the inside. And if I'm beautiful on the inside, the goodness will shine out and make me beautiful on the outside. Good night, God.

Silly Me

Do not be guilty of telling bad stories and of foolish talk. These things are not for you to do. Instead, you are to give thanks for what God has done for you.
EPHESIANS 5:4

God, sometimes I can be silly. At times I need to calm down. Sometimes, in the right setting, being a little silly is okay. But other times it's inappropriate. If I'm not careful, I can embarrass myself and my parents. That would make me feel really silly.

I like showing that I'm happy, but help me to find ways that I can show my joy without being silly or telling bad stories. Help me to have fun without being too loud or embarrassing myself.

Thank You for fun times and for things that make me and others happy. Good night, God.

Hear and See

The hearing ear and the seeing
eye were both made by the Lord.
PROVERBS 20:12

God, You've given me ears to hear and eyes to see.
But if I'm not listening, or if I have my eyes closed, I
can miss the things You want me to hear and see.
It might be listening to a friend who needs to share
something inside her heart or seeing someone
whom I can help and telling that person all the wonderful things about You.

Help me to keep my ears alert and my eyes open.
And help me to see all the good things in front of
me—good things that You have put there.

Thank You for being able to share what I hear
and see. And thank You for my ears and my eyes that
You made. Good night, God.

Little Children

Jesus called the followers to Him and said,
"Let the little children come to Me. Do
not try to stop them. The holy nation
of God is made up of ones like these.
For sure, I tell you, whoever does not
receive the holy nation of God as a child
will not go into the holy nation."
LUKE 18:16–17

God, I am so glad that You love children so very
much and that You don't want anyone to get in
the way or stop us from coming to You. In fact, You
even tell grown-ups that they should love You the
way we children do.

I guess it's because children love with pure
hearts. I know that as I get older, things will try to
take the high places where You sit in my heart now.
Please don't let me ever love anyone or anything
more than You.

Thank You for loving me and for loving children
as much as You do. Good night, God.

Broken Hearts

He heals those who have a broken
heart. He heals their sorrows.
PSALM 147:3

Things get broken—even friendships. I am sad and heartbroken when a friend and I don't get along. Losing a friend can hurt really badly. I don't want to do anything to hurt my friends. They mean too much to me. Good friends are a special gift from You, God.

You fix broken things—especially hearts. With Your help, broken friendships can be made right again. But first we both may have to be willing to say we're sorry. Then we never have to talk about what caused the problem again, and we can try to forget it ever happened.

Thank You, God, that You fix broken things like hearts and friendships. I know I can always come to You when my heart hurts. Good night, God.

God Is Not Slow

The Lord is not slow about keeping His promise as some people think. He is waiting for you. The Lord does not want any person to be punished forever. He wants all people to be sorry for their sins and turn from them.

2 PETER 3:9

God, You're not slow to keep Your promises. But You are willing to wait on me. Sometimes I'm slow. Especially when I need to talk to You about something that's bothering me. I guess I forget that You are always right there beside me, ready to help me no matter what my problem is.

Help me not to be slow about remembering that You are right there. I should come to You first to talk about anything and everything. Why wouldn't I? You know everything, and You care more about me than anybody. You are the One who created me and put me where I am.

God, thank You for not being slow to keep Your promises. And thank You for loving me even though I am often slow to think of You. Thank You, God, and good night.

Not Getting Caught

There is no joy while we are being punished.
It is hard to take, but later we can see
that good came from it. And it gives us
the peace of being right with God.
HEBREWS 12:11

Sometimes kids do bad things and get away with it.
Doing wrong seems to make them happy. But I feel
awful inside when I do something bad and don't get
caught. That feeling is called conviction, and You
let me feel it because You want me to ask for Your
forgiveness and do better next time.

I don't like getting caught, but I know it's for my
own good when I do. You don't let me get away with
much, God. That's because You love me. You want to
keep me close to You. It's the same when my parents
catch me doing something wrong. They punish me
because they love me.

Thank You for loving me enough to correct me.
And thank You for giving me parents who love me
that much too. Good night, God.

He Numbers the Stars

He knows the number of the stars.
He gives names to all of them.
PSALM 147:4

I love all the beautiful stars You made. There are so many that I could never count them all. Yet You know every single star. You don't just know how many there are—You give each one a name!

If You know the name of every star, then I know for sure that You know the name of every person who ever lived and will live. You are so amazing, God!

Thank You that I have all the wonderful stars to look at, Father. They remind me of how big You are and how marvelous it is that You know everything. Thank You for counting me and knowing my name. Good night, God.

Storybook Love

Be sure your love is true love. Hate what
is sinful. Hold on to whatever is good.
ROMANS 12:9

God, when I think of true love, I think of a handsome prince who rides up on a white stallion to save a beautiful maiden locked up in a dark castle. He loves her so much that he is willing to fight an evil king or a fire-breathing dragon. That's a storybook kind of love.

I think that's how You are, God. You have the true kind of love that is willing to fight evil to save me. That evil is sin, and Jesus fought and won that battle on the cross. He gave His life. And that's the biggest and best kind of true love.

I am so thankful that You sent Your Son, Jesus, who is my Prince, who came to save me from sin. Thank You, God, and good night.

God Understands

Great is our Lord, and great in power.
His understanding has no end.
PSALM 147:5

Sometimes I don't feel like I'm being understood.
It feels as if nobody knows exactly what's going on
with me. And explaining my feelings can be hard.

But You, God, are great! You are all-powerful,
above anything else in heaven or on earth. You know
every thought I have exactly when I'm thinking it—
even before I think it! Not only do You know what I'm
feeling, but You also understand me completely. You
are like no other.

I am so grateful that I serve a God who is all-
powerful and who understands all things. Thank
You, God, and good night.

Good Thinking

Christian brothers, keep your minds thinking about whatever is true, whatever is respected, whatever is right, whatever is pure, whatever can be loved, and whatever is well thought of. If there is anything good and worth giving thanks for, think about these things.

PHILIPPIANS 4:8

God, I don't always think about good things. Sometimes I think about something that's bad. I may think bad thoughts about kids I don't get along with or about getting even. Or I might think about how I can stay out of trouble by stretching the truth.

But I know that's not how I'm supposed to think. To have a peaceful and joyful life, I need to think about always telling the truth, always being respectful, and always doing whatever is right. I'm to think pure thoughts, not rude or dirty things. You want me to think about all the lovely things that are worth thinking about.

I always want to think like You think. Thank You, God, and good night.

Don't Bend

So stand up and do not be moved.
Wear a belt of truth around your
body. Wear a piece of iron over your
chest which is being right with God.
EPHESIANS 6:14

If I bend a plastic ruler too far, it will break. It wasn't
meant to be bendable. It was meant to make straight
lines. God's Word is that way. It wasn't meant to be
bent. And just as a ruler can give the true measure-
ment of something, so does God's Word.

Some people try to bend Your Word, God. But I
should never bend Your truth to make it say what I want
it to say. And when others are bending it, it's probably
because it keeps them from feeling guilty. But I know
that bending Your truth is breaking Your rules.

Thank You, God, for giving me rules that are not
to be broken. Thank You that Your words will always
stay straight, unbroken, and true. Good night, God.

Be Seen

All things can be seen when they
are in the light. Everything that
can be seen is in the light.
EPHESIANS 5:13

When I enter a dark room, I have the choice to turn on the light or stay in the dark. I could sit in the dark and no one would see me. Belonging to You can be like that. I can enter a room and never mention Your name. No one would know I am Yours.

But I don't want to live in the dark or enter a room and never mention Your name or tell someone about You. I want to turn on the light by sharing Your love with everyone I meet. I want everyone to see You in the light.

Thank You that I can turn on the light for others by sharing You. Being loved by You is the best thing that has ever happened to me, and I want to share You everywhere I go. Good night, God.

A Time for Everything

There is a special time for everything.
There is a time for everything
that happens under heaven.
ECCLESIASTES 3:1

You gave us seasons, God. There's fall, winter, spring, and summer. Every season the weather changes, and I can tell that by looking at the leaves. In the fall, they are beautiful yellows, oranges, and reds. As winter approaches, the leaves die, turn brown, and fall off the branches. Then spring comes and the little pale green buds poke their heads out. As the bright sun of summer beats down, the pale green of the leaves turns to a rich dark green. Seasons don't stay the same. Neither does life.

Just like seasons, there are times for me to be happy and times to be sad. Times for me to work and times for rest. I'm a kid now, but there will be a time for me to grow up.

Thank You for changing seasons, God. And thank You for a time to remember and a time to look forward to the future. Good night, God.

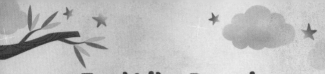

Feel Like Dancing

Let them praise His name with dancing. Let them sing praises to Him with timbrels and a harp.

PSALM 149:3

When I feel really happy, I like to dance. Joy isn't based on the things that are happening in my life. It comes from a place down deep inside me. I can have joy even when life isn't all rosy. And joyful is how I feel when I think about You, God. You bring so much joy to my heart. Joy! Joy! Joy!

And the reason I can feel so joyful is because Your Holy Spirit lives within me and makes me feel safe and loved. All I have to do is start praising You, God, and my heart feels light and my feet feel like dancing.

Thank You, Father, for the wonderful feelings of joy You put within me. And thank You that I can dance before You. I am thankful to be Your daughter. Good night, Father.

A Good Rest

And so my heart is glad. My soul
is full of joy. My body also
will rest without fear.

PSALM 16:9

Sometimes I'm afraid at night. I wake up and want to be near someone. Then I remember that I don't have to be afraid because You are always with me. You never leave me, and You never sleep.

When I do wake up and can't go back to sleep or I'm worrying about something or something makes me afraid, I can think on things that make me glad. I can think of the people who love me and thank You for giving them to me. I can sing songs that remind me of how much You love children and how much You love me. And before long, I am fast asleep again.

Thank You that my heart is glad and that I can be full of joy. Thank You that I don't have to be afraid, because You are always here. And thank You for a good rest. Good night, God.

Really, God?

So Sarah laughed to herself, saying, "Will I have this joy after my husband and I have grown old?" Then the Lord said to Abraham, "Why did Sarah laugh and say, 'How can I give birth to a child when I am so old?' Is anything too hard for the Lord? I will return to you at this time next year, and Sarah will have a son."

GENESIS 18:12–14

Abraham's wife, Sarah, was an old lady when You told her that she would become a mom. In fact, she was old enough to be a grandmother. The idea of it made her laugh. Sarah must have thought having a baby in her old age was a huge joke. She was ninety years old, way too old to have a baby. But she did. She had a son named Isaac. I guess You got the last laugh, God.

Sarah had always wanted a child but could never have one. But You gave her what she wanted most in the world. When You do mysterious things, You can bring a lot of happiness.

Help me never to laugh when You say You're going to do the impossible. Nothing is impossible with You, God. Thank You, and good night.

Family

From now on you are not strangers and
people who are not citizens. You are
citizens together with those who belong
to God. You belong in God's family.
EPHESIANS 2:19

God, some kids don't have traditional families.
Some live with their grandparents, an aunt, or
an uncle. Some kids are adopted. But even when
people grow up without a family, that doesn't mean
they have to be alone. Because when You adopt
people intoYour family, they get to be part of a
really *big* family—Your family. And that's a family
we will live with forever and ever. I'm happy that
I am part of the family of God and I won't ever be
completely alone.

Thank You for my family whom I live with and for
Your big family, God. And thank You that I belong to
You. Good night, God.

My Heart Sings

Praise the Lord! For it is good to sing praises to our God. For it is pleasing and praise is right.

PSALM 147:1

I love to sing! Especially about happy things. You like me to sing about You, God. It's pleasing to Your ears. You don't even care how I sound. I may sing off-key, but You hear what's in my heart. I'm glad You can hear what's in my heart.

And I'm glad that You think it's good to sing praises to You. It's fun to make up songs to tell You how much I love You. I bet those are Your favorite songs to hear.

Thank You for songs and for music. Singing songs about You makes me especially happy. I know those are the songs that put a smile on Your face. Thank You, and good night, God.

Bouquet of Flowers

Nothing should be done because of pride or thinking about yourself. Think of other people as more important than yourself.

PHILIPPIANS 2:3

God, my parents, teachers, and coaches sometimes tell me that they are proud of me because I have done something well. But if I didn't have good teachers and coaches, I couldn't do good work. I shouldn't have pride in myself, because You are the one who gave me a good mind that can learn and people who care enough about me to teach me.

If someone gave me a bouquet of flowers for doing a good job, I think it would be nice to take some of the flowers and give them to the ones who helped me. That way I'm not taking all the credit, but I would be sharing the joy.

Thank You, God, for those who help me do good work and for the people in my life who want me to succeed. Good night.

The Fun of Art

But now, O Lord, You are our Father. We are the clay, and You are our pot maker. All of us are the work of Your hand.

ISAIAH 64:8

It's fun to create things. I like to draw, color, and make things out of playdough. Creating makes me feel like an artist. You are an artist too, God. You created everything that's on the earth with Your hands. You created people of all kinds, animals that walk and crawl, birds that fly or wobble on the ground, and fish that swim and float. You made every plant, flower, and tree on the earth. You made so many beautiful and unusual things. And You made me.

I'm glad You are such a good artist. Thank You for all the things that are the works of Your hands. Good night, God.

Making Plans

There are many plans in a man's heart,
but it is the Lord's plan that will stand.
PROVERBS 19:21

God, sometimes I make plans. But if something goes wrong and things don't turn out the way I want them to, I can get upset. I can be disappointed. And that doesn't feel good.

I know it's okay to make plans. But if they don't work out the way I hoped, I should try to see the good in all of it. It may be that You, God, have something different planned for me. It may even be better than what I hoped for.

God, help me to let go of my plans and be willing to do things someone else's way. It just might be that it will be even more fun doing things that way. And it may be that it will be awesome because it's done Your way. Thank You, and good night!

God's Favor

The Lord was sorry that He had made man on the earth. He had sorrow in His heart. So the Lord said, "I will destroy man whom I have made from the land, man and animals, things that move upon the earth and birds of the sky. For I am sorry that I have made them." But Noah found favor in the eyes of the Lord.

GENESIS 6:6–8

God, when I obey You, I find favor in Your eyes. You were able to save the world through one man because he found favor in Your eyes by obeying all that You asked him to do.

You told Noah to build an ark—a *huge* boat. It took him a long, long time to build it. Everyone pointed at him and laughed. But Noah kept on building and obeying You, God.

You can do great things through people who obey You. I want You to be able to do great things through me too, God. Thank You, and good night.

Queen Esther

"For if you keep quiet at this time, help will come to the Jews from another place. But you and your father's house will be destroyed. Who knows if you have not become queen for such a time as this?"

ESTHER 4:14

God, Esther became a queen at a time when girls didn't have much say about the way things were done. Even grown girls. But You used Esther to save her family and her whole nation. You put her in King Xerxes's kingdom and gave her a good relationship with her husband. There she could help him to see the evil people who were trying to hurt her people. You gave her a voice and the chance to speak to the king.

I want to be like Queen Esther. I want to use my voice to help others, God. Just as You had a purpose for her, You have a purpose for me too.

Help me to be ready and willing to speak up when You want me to, Father. I know You put me exactly where I am for a purpose. Help me to be like Esther. Thank You, God. Good night!

Hear Me, God

The Lord will not hear me if I hold on to
sin in my heart. But it is sure that God
has heard. He has listened to the voice of
my prayer. Honor and thanks be to God!
He has not turned away from my prayer
or held His loving-kindness from me.
PSALM 66:18–20

God, I want You to always hear me when I talk to
You. I know I need to make sure that I have told You
about all the bad things I have done. And I need to be
willing to stop doing the things that I know are wrong.

Being honest with You is important. That way I
can know that You are listening to me. It will be hard
to share all the things that I have done because I
know sometimes I let You down. But if I want You to
hear the good stuff, I need to be willing to tell You
the bad stuff too.

Help me to be completely honest and open with
You, God. I know that You will understand and forgive
me for anything if I ask. Thank You, and good night.

Thrones

Christ has gone to heaven and is on the
right side of God. Angels and powers
of heaven are obeying Him.
1 PETER 3:22

It's so wonderful, Father God, that Jesus is in heaven with You. He sits to the right of Your throne because He is royalty—King Jesus, the Son of God. And there are angels with You in heaven. Angels are Your messengers, and they obey Your every word.

I know that someday I will see King Jesus sitting on His throne right next to You. How wonderful that will be! Heaven will be perfect because You and Jesus will be there.

I'm glad Your Son is sitting next to You. Thank You, God, that someday everyone will know that You and Jesus have all the power in heaven and on earth. Good night, God.

Gold Test

"But He knows the way that I take. When He has tried me, I will come out as gold."

JOB 23:10

Teachers give students tests. They aren't fun, but tests are one way teachers can tell if we have understood what they have taught us. That makes tests important. You give tests too, God. Not the kind with a pencil and paper. Your tests are about whether we are willing to obey You.

Abraham and Sarah were told to leave their country, their home, and their family. You wanted to give Abraham and Sarah some new land and make them a great nation. They obeyed You and left their family as You told them to do. You blessed them for believing what You told them.

God, You test me too. You test me to see if I believe what You tell me. I pass Your test when I obey what You tell me to do. Help me always to obey You and pass Your test, God. Thank You, and good night.

You Send Angels

Praise the Lord, you powerful
angels of His who do what He says,
obeying His voice as He speaks!

PSALM 103:20

Angels are beautiful and powerful. You created them, and they are Your messengers, God. They obey Your voice. You send angels to bring good news to earth.

In fact, You sent an angel to tell Mary she would give birth to a son, the Most High God, King Jesus. Angels appeared to the shepherds in the field by night. Angels were also there to worship Jesus when He was born. They gave Jesus strength when He was on earth as a grown man.

You send angels to protect and help Your children too, God. They are always praising You. And I praise You too. Thank You, and good night, God.

My Part in a Play

Our own body has many parts.
When all these many parts are put
together, they are only one body.
The body of Christ is like this.

1 CORINTHIANS 12:12

Acting in a play is fun. I get to learn lines and pretend I am a character in the play. But I can only act in one part. Others are needed to put on a play. When we put all the parts together, it runs smoothly and the play is done well. And no one gets worn out from having too many parts.

Being in the family of God is like being in a play—everybody has one part to play. There is enough work for everyone without someone having to do it all. Everyone works together, and no one has to work alone.

I'm glad there are many parts in Your body of believers, God. And it makes me happy to know that we're working together toward one goal: to make You known to the world. Thank You, and good night, God.

Making Lemonade

"You planned to do a bad thing to me.
But God planned it for good, to make
it happen that many people should
be kept alive, as they are today."

GENESIS 50:20

God, jealousy can make people do bad things. Joseph had eleven brothers. His father, Jacob, gave him a beautiful coat of many colors. That made his older brothers jealous. They were so envious that they took his coat and threw him into a deep well.

But God, You saved Joseph out of the hole and gave him a job in the kingdom in Egypt. Soon Joseph became powerful. Years later his brothers came to him in Egypt to buy food because there was a famine in the land where they lived. Because Joseph was powerful, he was able to help his brothers. Even though they had treated him very badly, he saved them. He turned lemons into lemonade.

Thank You, God, that You can take me out of bad places and put me into places where I can be a help to others. Even if it's people who have done bad things to me, help me be willing to forgive. Then I can turn lemons into lemonade. Good night, God.

Who Do You Listen To?

But Rehoboam turned away from
the wise words the leaders gave him.
Instead he spoke with the young men who
grew up with him and stood by him.

1 KINGS 12:8

King Rehoboam did evil. He didn't set his heart to seek You, God. He was foolish. He went to his friends, who he knew would just tell him what he wanted to hear, when he should have been listening to the wise, older leaders.

Sometimes, God, I listen to my friends instead of listening to my parents or other adults. Usually it's because I want to do the fun, easy things my friends like to do. But I know that I need to be willing to ask and listen to wiser people like my parents when I have difficult decisions to make. That way I won't make bad or silly mistakes.

I don't want to be foolish like Rehoboam. Thank You for putting wise people in my life who care for me, God. I know that I can talk to them about anything. Help me to listen with open ears and a willing heart. Thank You, and good night, God.

Who I Look Like

And God made man in His own likeness.
In the likeness of God He made him.
He made both male and female.
GENESIS 1:27

God, some kids look like their moms, and some kids look like their dads. And some kids don't look like anybody they're related to. It's fun trying to figure out who I look like. But we all look like You because You created us in Your image. You wanted a family who looks like You.

You made us to have brains so we can think and make decisions. And You gave us bodies with legs so that we can walk and arms so that we can hold things and hug people. You even gave us mouths and tongues so we can talk and eat. Your Word says that I am fearfully and wonderfully made. I am made in Your image.

Thank You, God, for making me in Your image. And Thank You that Jesus is the perfect image of You. Good night, God.

Rules

So the Lord God sent him out from the garden of Eden, to work the ground from which he was taken. So He drove the man out. And He placed cherubim east of the garden of Eden with a sword of fire that turned every way. They kept watch over the path to the tree of life.

GENESIS 3:23–24

God, when I disobey, my parents have to punish me. They don't want to, but they do it to protect me. They have to set rules so that I can know what my limits are. If I had a puppy, I couldn't just let it run loose. Because I would love my puppy, I'd put a fence around it to protect and keep it safe.

You are like that too, God. You gave Adam and Eve rules to protect them. You told them not to eat the fruit from the one tree in the garden that would hurt them. But they disobeyed and ate the fruit. You had to make them leave the Garden of Eden to save them.

Thank You for giving me rules that keep me safe and for parents who love me enough to put up fences. When they punish me, I know it's because they love me. Good night, God.

A Good Daughter

She makes herself ready with strength,
and makes her arms strong. She sees
that what she has earned is good. Her
lamp does not go out at night.

PROVERBS 31:17–18

God, I want to be a good daughter. When I grow up, I want to be the kind of woman You want me to be. Kind, helpful, and loving.

I want to grow up strong and be willing to work hard. To be creative and use my hands to make beautiful things that I can share with others. And to be loving to my family and make a good home for them. To always think of others. And whatever I do, to be a blessing to all.

God, someday I will be the kind of woman who honors You and wants to please You. Thank You for showing me what kind of grown-up You want me to be. Good night, God.

Don't Be Lazy

Being lazy makes one go into a
deep sleep, and a lazy man will
suffer from being hungry.
PROVERBS 19:15

Sometimes I can be lazy, God. I don't feel like doing anything. But I know You don't want me to be like that all the time. You gave us a time to rest and a time to work.

If nobody ever worked, we would all go hungry. People have to work together so that they can help each other. Maybe it's a job or maybe it's chores, but You want people to be busy. Life can't be all fun and games all the time.

God, help me to offer to help my mom or dad. I know that it pleases You for me to stay busy. Helping around the house or working for my neighbors is good for me. Help me learn to be a good worker so that I will never go hungry. Thank You, and good night, God.

Lost and Found

"What if a woman has ten silver pieces of money and loses one of them? Does she not light a lamp and sweep the floor and look until she finds it? When she finds it, she calls her friends and neighbors together. She says to them, 'Be happy with me. I have found the piece of money I had lost.'"

LUKE 15:8–9

When the woman lost her silver piece, she cleaned and swept until she found it. And when she found it, she was so happy that she called her friends and neighbors to let them know it had been found, and to rejoice with her. I'm happy she found it, just as I'm happy when I find something I've lost.

You feel that way too, God. And the thing most valuable to You is people. You want them to choose to follow You. When they don't, You will search everywhere to find them.

I'm glad that You think people are valuable. That You will search and search to find us. Thank You, and good night, God.

Be the Example

Let no one show little respect for
you because you are young. Show other
Christians how to live by your life. They
should be able to follow you in the way you
talk and in what you do. Show them how to
live in faith and in love and in holy living.

1 TIMOTHY 4:12

God, I like it when I can help others, especially my mom or dad. When I do a good job and do what I'm told, it makes it easier for adults to ask me to do helpful things later. And if other kids are watching me, they'll see that I've been obedient. I need to show that obeying is important for everyone.

Thank You, God, for using me. Especially if it has to do with helping someone in need or telling someone about You. I want everyone to see Jesus through me. He's the only One who lived a perfect and obedient life.

Thank You, God, for Jesus who shows all kids how to live. Good night, God.

My Parents Love Me So Much

But the time came when she could hide him no longer. So she took a basket made from grass, and covered it with tar and put the child in it. And she set it in the grass by the side of the Nile.

EXODUS 2:3

Moses' mother loved him so much that she was willing to give him up to keep him safe. Moms do hard things for their kids. Moses was a baby, and his mom bundled him up and put him in a basket in the long grass at the edge of the Nile River. You saw him floating there and protected him, God. You led an Egyptian princess to find him floating in the river. She took him into her home and raised him.

God, You use the love that moms and dads have for their kids to take care of us. They even love me enough to read to me about You. They want me to grow up and have a happy life because I know You, God.

Thank You for my parents' love. Help me to let them know how much it means to me that they will do anything to keep me safe. Good night, God.

Some Things Never Change

The grass dries up. The flower loses its color.
But the Word of our God stands forever.

ISAIAH 40:8

Flowers are beautiful. But they don't last forever. When it gets cold, the flowers go away. The leaves turn from green to bright yellows, oranges, and reds. Then they fall off the trees. There are some things that can change, but not what's in the Bible. The Bible never changes because it's Your Word, God.

I like that I never have to worry that the Bible will change. It's good for me to learn while I'm young and all throughout my life, even as an old lady. While the flowers will wilt and the leaves will fall, You tell me that Your Word stands forever! And that's a super-long time.

Thank You, God, that Your Word never changes, because that means that I can trust every word in the Bible. Good night, God.

Just a Kid

Josiah did what is right in the eyes
of the Lord. He walked in all the way
of his father David. He did not turn
aside to the right or to the left.

2 KINGS 22:2

Even though I'm young, God, I can influence people.
Josiah was eight years old when he became a king.
There has never been a king, before or after, quite
like Josiah. He had the doorkeepers of the temple
collect money to repair the temple, and he hired
carpenters and masons to do the work. When the
high priest discovered the Book of the Law in the
temple, Josiah discovered that the people had not
been obeying Your law. He repented for their sin.
He tore down the altars to false gods and got rid of
the devil worshippers. This kept You from having to
punish the people during Josiah's reign. King Josiah
learned how important Your rules are. I am learning
the same thing!

Thank You, God, for kids You used in the Bible.
And thank You for using me. Good night.

Special Gifts

See, children are a gift from the Lord. The children born to us are our special reward.

PSALM 127:3

Who doesn't love getting gifts? I sure do. But God, You say that I *am* a gift. A gift from You to my family. Gifts make me feel good. I'm glad that my arrival into the world made my family feel good. And it makes me feel super special to think that I am Your gift. I want to always be the gift that keeps making my family feel good.

You give all babies as gifts. But You gave the whole world a very special baby—Jesus, and He grew up and gave His life so that He could make the whole world feel good.

Thank You for making me a special gift, and especially for giving the world the gift of baby Jesus. Good night, God.

Grandparents Are the Best, God!

Grandchildren are the pride
and joy of old men and a
son is proud of his father.

PROVERBS 17:6

Grandparents are the best! They think about me,
cheer for me when I play games, and come to watch
any activity I participate in. They play with me, remember my birthday, and treat me extra special.
They laugh at all my jokes—even if my jokes aren't
very funny. They love me in very special ways.

I want to always make my grandparents proud
of me. I'd never want to do anything to embarrass
them or make them sad. I want to bring them only
joy. There's nothing better than when I'm the one
who gets to put a smile on their faces.

Thank You, God, for grandparents and for all the
special ways they love me and show me they care.
And thank You for making grandparents the best,
God. Good night.

First to See

It was early on the first day of the week when Jesus was raised from the dead. Mary Magdalene saw Him first. He had put seven demons out of her.

MARK 16:9

God, Your Son was killed and buried in a tomb. Because He is God, He defeated the devil and sin forever. He rose from the grave! The first person to see Jesus alive again was a girl! Mary Magdalene had been a follower of Jesus when He was on earth. She loved Jesus very much because He did some awesome things to make her well again. He healed her *and* saved her.

It's so cool that the first person Jesus appeared to was a girl! You love girls a lot, God. And You make us feel important in Your sight. I'm glad that I'm a girl who is important to You. Thank You for Mary Magdalene and for giving her the honor of seeing You first. Good night, God.

You Love Animals, God

There is the wide sea full of both large and small animals. There are too many for us to number. The ships sail there. And the very large sea animal You have made plays in it. They all wait for You to give them their food at the right time. You give it to them and they gather it up. You open Your hand and they are filled with good things.
PSALM 104:25–28

You love animals, God, and so do I. A pet can seem like a part of my family, even if it has fur or feathers. Pets play with me and lick my face to show me that they love me. I think animals are some of the very best things You made.

You take care of the animals that live on land and in water. You made sure they would have places to live and food to eat. I can help You by feeding my pets, taking them for walks, petting them, and being kind to them.

I'm glad You love animals like I do. Thank You for making animals, and thank You for pets. Good night, God.

Enough to Go Around

When they were filled, Jesus said to His followers, "Gather up the pieces that are left. None will be wasted." The followers gathered the pieces together. Twelve baskets were filled with pieces of barley bread. These were left after all the people had eaten.

JOHN 6:12–13

God, You never let Your children be in need. When Jesus was traveling around and preaching, huge crowds followed Him. Once when the crowd got hungry, Jesus used a boy's lunch of five small loaves of bread and two fish to feed everyone in the crowd. No one went hungry. In fact, they had twelve full baskets of bread and fish left over!

Jesus cared that the crowd was hungry. And even though He only had a basket full of food, He made it enough to go around. That's how Your love is, God. You're more than enough for me and the whole world. I will never feel unloved or uncared for as long as I stay close to You.

It makes me happy to think that You are enough for me and that You think about all my needs. Thank You, God, and good night.

Stepparents

While he was thinking about this, an angel
of the Lord came to him in a dream. The
angel said, "Joseph, son of David, do not be
afraid to take Mary as your wife. She is to
become a mother by the Holy Spirit. A Son
will be born to her. You will give Him the
name Jesus because He will save His people
from the punishment of their sins."

MATTHEW 1:20–21

God, there are lots of kids who have stepdads or
stepmoms. Even though they're not the parents who
were there when they were born, stepparents still
love their stepchildren.

Joseph was a stepdad to Jesus. Joseph watched
over Jesus when He was a baby and took really
good care of Him. An angel even came to Joseph
and told him not to be afraid to take Mary as his
wife. The angel told Joseph to name the baby Jesus.
Joseph was told that his stepson, Jesus, would save
His people and the whole world from their sins.

Stepparents have a very special place in a kid's
life. Please bless each one. Good night, God.

Little Ray of Sunshine

Put out of your life all these things: bad
feelings about other people, anger, temper,
loud talk, bad talk which hurts other people,
and bad feelings which hurt other people.
You must be kind to each other. Think of
the other person. Forgive other people
just as God forgave you because of
Christ's death on the cross.

EPHESIANS 4:31–32

God, nobody likes a grumble bunny. They make
everybody miserable, and they take all the fun out
of everything. I don't want to be a grumble bunny. I
want to make people happy. I want people to enjoy
being around me. That means I need to watch out
for bad thoughts. I need to be careful not to say
anything hurtful.

I want to be like sunshine. Sunshine is good for
people, and it makes me happy. If I have sunshine
in my heart, that means that I'm going to have a
nice day—even if it rains. When I'm thankful and not
grumbly, I can be a ray of sunshine.

Thank You, God, that I can be sunshine even on
a cloudy day. Good night.

Show Kindness

And one of you says to him, "Goodbye,
keep yourself warm and eat well."
But if you do not give him what he
needs, how does that help him?

JAMES 2:16

I like being kind to others. It makes me feel good inside. Being kind means that I put my good feelings toward others into action.

If I saw someone who was hungry and told them to eat well but didn't offer them any food, what good would I have done? And what if they were cold and I told them to be warm but didn't offer them a jacket? How would my words have helped keep them from feeling hungry or helped them to stay warm? Good words, without good acts, are empty. They aren't worth anything.

Help me to be willing to show kindness through my actions and to share what I can with those in need. Thank You, God, for letting me see when my words are empty. Good night!

A Good Friend

Four men came to Jesus carrying a man who could not move his body. These men could not get near Jesus because of so many people. They made a hole in the roof of the house over where Jesus stood. Then they let down the bed with the sick man on it.

MARK 2:3–4

If I had a friend who got hurt, I would take them to someone I knew could help them and would care about making them well again. That's just what the friends of a paralyzed man did—they lowered him down through the roof to put him in front of Jesus because they knew that Jesus would take care of him.

Those are the kinds of friends I would want. And that's exactly the kind of friend I want to be. I know I can bring anyone or anything to You, God. Even though You are super busy, You will always have time for me and my friends.

You are a God who is ready to help. Thank You, and good night, God.

You Gave Us Pets

Then God said, "Let Us make man like Us and let him be head over the fish of the sea, and over the birds of the air, and over the cattle, and over all the earth, and over every thing that moves on the ground."

GENESIS 1:26

People own pets. Pets don't own people. That's because You made people smarter than animals, God. You put people in charge of all creation.

Everything was put here for us. The land grows and supplies food. The sea also provides food and minerals. The rain gives us fresh water to drink and take baths in. You even made the air for us to breathe. You thought of everything, God!

I'm glad that pets don't own people. That wouldn't work out well. Thank You for putting people over Your creation. Help me to be a good caretaker of all the wonderful things You created. Thank You, God. Good night.

Thankful Music

Tell of your joy to each other by singing
the Songs of David and church songs. Sing
in your heart to the Lord. Always give
thanks for all things to God the Father
in the name of our Lord Jesus Christ.
EPHESIANS 5:19–20

Music has a beat and notes, and most music has
words. Together they make a beautiful sound. Joy
and kindness can be like sweet music. The beat is
the beating heart of a kind, caring person. Add to
that the words of one who is thankful. And the notes
are the sounds that come from a joyful place of
knowing You, God.

I want to sing beautiful songs of thanksgiving
and kindness every day. I will sing in my heart to You,
God. I have so much to be thankful for. I hope my
thanksgiving and kindness are music to Your ears.

Thank You for hearing the songs that I sing to
You in my heart, God. Good night.

Time to Bake

Love takes everything that comes without giving up. Love believes all things. Love hopes for all things. Love keeps on in all things.

1 CORINTHIANS 13:7

Pride can keep me from meeting a new friend. So can fear. Trying to make friends can be scary because I don't always know if someone wants to be my friend. My feelings would be hurt if they didn't. But that doesn't mean that I should give up trying to be a friend.

You say that love doesn't give up, God. I think that means not giving up on making a new friend too. Just like when my mom bakes a cake, it takes time. It needs time to bake to be delicious. Some of the best things don't happen all at once. Some friendships may have to "bake" too.

Help me to be patient while I wait for a new friendship to bake. And thank You for the friendships that turn out to be delicious. Good night, God.

Written on My Heart

"This is the New Way of Worship that I will give to the Jews. When that day comes," says the Lord, "I will put My Law into their minds. And I will write it on their hearts. I will be their God, and they will be My people."
JEREMIAH 31:33

Sometimes, God, I wish I had just the right words to say. It would be nice to know what You want me to say. I know that You want me to understand and memorize what's in the Bible. But I have trouble memorizing verses sometimes. You have told me to write Your words on my heart. And that means knowing what they mean.

I want to learn Your Word. Saying verses from the Bible out loud is a great way to write them on my heart. That way, when I need to remember a verse, it will come to my mind quickly.

I am thankful for Your Word and for minds that can memorize. Please help me to understand what Your words mean. Thank You, God. Good night.

Ears to Listen

Be at peace with all men. Live a
holy life. No one will see the Lord
without having that kind of life.

HEBREWS 12:14

It's hard not to disagree every now and then. But it's not fun when I'm having an argument with a friend. It can lead to doing things that I wish I hadn't. And that's not a good feeling at all.

You want me to get along with everyone. That may mean that sometimes I need to let others have their way, or even tell a friend that I was wrong. That can be hard to do, but I know that You will help me do it if I ask You.

You want me to live in peace with everyone, God. I know that You will give me what I need to be able to do that. When I let You, You can shut my mouth so that my ears can listen. It's You who makes my heart ready to hear what others have to say. And You help me to stand in their shoes. Thank You, God. Good night.

Belonging

But now the Lord Who made you, O Jacob,
and He Who made you, O Israel, says,
"Do not be afraid. For I have bought
you and made you free. I have called
you by name. You are Mine!"

ISAIAH 43:1

I have things that belong to me—the things in my
room, such as toys, clothes, books, and stuff. I can
do almost anything I want with my stuff—*almost*—
because it belongs to me.

I belong to my parents. They are in charge of
what I do. They take care of things that concern me
so that I don't have to. I'm glad they do.

I also belong to You, God. And because I do, You
take care of the big things in my life so that I don't
have to. That's really good, because I don't always
understand the big things.

Thank You, God, for making the big decision to
put me into my family. And thank You for parents
who make good decisions for me. Good night, God.

Upside-Down Frown

A glad heart makes a happy face, but when
the heart is sad, the spirit is broken.
PROVERBS 15:13

When I'm upset, I frown. A frown is really nothing but an upside-down smile. But when my heart is sad, it's hard to smile. A smile is like a cold; I can pass it on. But a smile is good and doesn't make me feel bad or cause me to sneeze.

I know I can always come to You when my heart is sad. You don't want me to be unhappy, God. I can come to You anytime and tell You about all the things that are making me unhappy. And after I talk to You, I can let them go and move on to happy thoughts and a happy face.

I'm glad smiles don't have to stay upside down, God. Smiles feel a lot better than frowns. They are nicer to look at too. Thank You, God, for smiles. Good night.

Sleepy and Grumpy

I will lie down and sleep in peace.
O Lord, You alone keep me safe.
PSALM 4:8

When I'm sleepy, I can be grumpy. I drag around and have no energy. That's because You made my body to rest every day. You knew that my body would need new energy.

Help me not to fight going to sleep. Help me to know when I need to stop playing and close my eyes. That way I can get the rest I need so that I can feel good the next morning.

Thank You, God, for sleep that keeps sleepy-and-grumpy me away. And for good rest that helps me to rise early and ready for a fun day. Good night, God.

Teach Me

I will show you and teach you in the
way you should go. I will tell you
what to do with My eye upon you.
PSALM 32:8

I go to school to learn. My teachers teach me how to do things—things that are important for me to know. I don't want to be lost and have no clue about what to do. That's why I have teachers and books to learn from.

It's the same with the Bible. The Bible teaches me how to not get lost and stray away from You, God. It teaches me how to live to please You. You know just what teaching I need and when I need it. So it's important for me to listen to teachers who teach me about You.

Thank You for teachers who teach me the important things in life, especially for the ones who teach me about You. Help me to always be ready to listen and learn. Thank You, God. Good night.

Rocks Will Cry Out!

Jesus said to them, "I tell you
that if these did not speak, the
very stones would call out."

LUKE 19:40

I've never heard a rock shout. That would be super weird! You made *people* to worship You. You expect us to sing and shout about how very wonderful You are. But if we don't, the rocks will cry out.

It seems sad to think that people wouldn't praise You, that it would be left to rocks to sing and shout out how great You are. I don't want a rock to take my place. I want to be the one to praise You, to sing and shout about how wonderful You are.

You are great, and I will sing and shout how wonderful You are all my life. Thank You, God, and good night.

Parting Waters

Then Moses put out his hand over the sea. And the Lord moved the sea all night by a strong east wind. So the waters were divided. And the people of Israel went through the sea on dry land. The waters were like a wall to them on their right and on their left.

EXODUS 14:21–22

When the people of Israel were being chased by the Egyptian pharaoh's army, You led them to camp by the Red Sea. They were terrified. No way could they swim across an entire sea. You told them not to worry because You had a plan. And Your plan was amazing! You parted the Red Sea so that the entire nation of Israel could walk through on dry land. Men, women, children, cattle, oxen, and sheep all got to the other side, safe and dry.

When You tell people to do something, You will do whatever it takes to help them do it—even wondrous things like holding back huge bodies of water containing all kinds of fish and sea life. You do great big things to save Your people.

Thank You, God, for rescuing Your people. Good night.

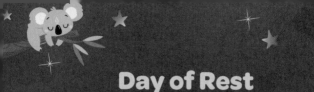

Day of Rest

Then God honored the seventh day and made it holy, because in it He rested from all His work which He had done.

GENESIS 2:3

God, You made it so that there would be seven days in a week. But the seventh day was extra special. You called it the Sabbath, which means "rest." When you created the earth, You rested on the seventh day. Today the Jewish people still worship You on Saturday, the seventh day of the week. But ever since Jesus rose from the dead on a Sunday, Christians take a Sabbath rest on Sunday. That doesn't mean that we are supposed to sleep all day. It means that rather than working to make a living, people can rest and spend the day worshipping You, thinking about You, and reading Your Word.

You knew that mankind needed a day to stop all our busyness to pause and focus on our relationship with You, God. Thank You, and good night, God.

Water from a Rock

The Lord said to Moses, "Pass in front of
the people and take some of the leaders
of Israel with you. Take the special stick
in your hand with which you hit the Nile,
and go. See, I will stand before you there
on the rock at Horeb. When you hit the
rock, water will come out of it and the
people will drink." And Moses did so.

EXODUS 17:5–6

If I were in a desert, I would get thirsty. It's hot and
dry in the desert. You can go for miles and miles and
never find fresh water to drink. When Your people
were in the wilderness, there was no place to find
water, God. You heard Your people cry out and led
them to a rock. You told Moses to strike it with a
stick, and when he did, water gushed out.

You hear our cries, God, and always come ready
to help. You can satisfy the thirst of all who are thirsty
for You. You never leave Your people wanting.

Thank You for hearing Your people's cries. Good
night, God.

Beauty from Within

Pleasing ways lie and beauty comes
to nothing, but a woman who
fears the Lord will be praised.
PROVERBS 31:30

Beauty doesn't last forever, God. And some girls who are pretty on the outside are not so pretty on the inside. In fact, they can be unpleasant to be around. But a girl who is pretty on the inside is beautiful to You, God. She is thoughtful, kind, wise, and giving. She is a joy to be around.

I want this kind of beauty, God. I want to be a joy to be around and not empty headed and full of silly ideas.

Thank You, God, for wisdom that makes me thoughtful, kind, and giving. Help my life to be inwardly beautiful. Good night, God.

On Your Mind

Your thoughts are of great worth to me,
O God. How many there are! If I could
number them, there would be more than
the sand. When I awake, I am still with You.
PSALM 139:17–18

I don't know how many grains of sand there are on the seashore. But there are a whole lot! So many that it's impossible to count them all. But the Bible says that You have more thoughts than there are grains of sand on the seashore. I think a lot of things during the day, God, but not enough to fill even a tiny cup with sand. And because You have so many thoughts, there's nothing new that You haven't thought of.

Sometimes I think about silly stuff. But none of Your thoughts are silly. I want to have more of Your thoughts and fewer of my silly thoughts.

I'm glad that I don't have to know everything You're thinking, God. Your thoughts are something that only You know how to deal with. Thank You for all the many things that You think about, and that one of those things is me. Good night, God.

My Safe Place

Because you have made the Lord your
safe place, and the Most High the place
where you live, nothing will hurt you.
No trouble will come near your tent.
For He will tell His angels to care for
you and keep you in all your ways.

PSALM 91:9–11

When I'm afraid, I look for my parents to run to.
They watch over me and make sure I'm safe. That's
because they love me, and they don't want anything
to happen to me. They give me a safe home to live
in. They are my safe place.

I can run to You too, God. You are my safe place.
And You are even bigger and stronger than my parents. You see everything, and You send Your angels
to watch over and protect me.

I'm glad that You put people in my life to protect
me. My parents are always close for me to run to,
and so are You. Thank You for giving me safe places,
God. Good night.

A Brave Lady

So the young men who had spied out the land went in, and brought out Rahab and her father and mother and brothers and all she had. They brought out all of her family and took them outside the tents of Israel.

JOSHUA 6:23

There are some brave women in the Bible, God. Rahab was one of them. She hid two of Your men when they were spying out her city and saved their lives. In return, Joshua's army spared Rahab and her family when they came to destroy Jericho.

Rahab had heard of Your power and feared You, God. Because of that, she helped Your people. You gave her credit for that and saved her life and gave her a new home with Your people. Even though Joshua's men were strangers to her, she risked a lot to help them do Your work. She was very courageous. She is a great example of how You can use anyone.

I'm glad there were courageous women in Bible times. They show me that I can be courageous too.

Thank You, God, and good night.

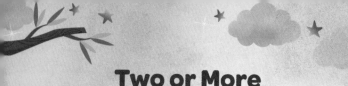

Two or More

"Again I tell you this: If two of you agree on earth about anything you pray for, it will be done for you by My Father in heaven. For where two or three are gathered together in My name, there I am with them."

MATTHEW 18:19–20

Praying is one of the most important things I can do. It's talking to You, God. Sometimes I pray about everyday things. But there are times when I pray about something that is very important. It may even be a prayer for someone else.

There are times when I need to pray with someone. You tell me that when two or more agree on something through prayer, that You will be there. That helps make my prayers very powerful. And it's easier to pray for something when I have someone to pray with.

Help me to find others to pray with, especially when I'm praying about something really important. It's good to know that others are praying with me. And thank You for always being in our midst. Good night, God.

Pride

He said, "Look! I see four men loose and walking about in the fire without being hurt! And the fourth one looks like a son of the gods (or the Son of God)!"

DANIEL 3:25

King Nebuchadnezzar was a prideful man. He was so impressed with himself that he had a ninety-foot-tall statue of himself made out of pure gold. That's a lot of gold! But pride is a bad thing, God. King Nebuchadnezzar made a rule that everyone had to bow down to his image. There were three boys—Shadrach, Meshach, and Abed-nego—who would not bow down to the image. They made the king so angry that he had them tied up and thrown into a hot, fiery furnace.

But a fourth person appeared in the furnace. That person was the Son of God. The boys were saved, and King Nebuchadnezzar was terrified. His pride couldn't save him. The king realized that You are a God to be feared.

Thank You, God, for saving those who bow down to You alone. Good night, God.

You See Everything

Even before I speak a word,
O Lord, You know it all.
PSALM 139:4

When I do something bad, I sometimes try to hide it. I don't want to get into trouble for doing something I know is wrong. At times I can hide it for a while, but I usually get caught.

You see *everything*, God. I can't hide anything from You. You can see to and through anything. But there are times when I'd like to hide things from You—something bad that I've done or said. But there's nowhere to hide. I don't even have to say a word because You already know.

That's why I need to tell You myself when I've done something wrong. It's best if I tell You as soon as I've done it; then I won't feel bad all day long. Thank You for being someone I can come to even when I'd rather hide. Good night, God.

Telling Secrets

He who is always telling stories makes secrets known, but he who can be trusted keeps a thing hidden.
PROVERBS 11:13

Sometimes my friends tell me secrets. I have to be careful with secrets because some secrets about others I shouldn't listen to. I should just say, "No, thanks," and walk away. Especially if it's something bad about someone or something I don't have any business knowing anything about. But if I do hear it, then I shouldn't tell anyone else. It's not my secret to tell.

Forgive me, God, when I share secrets that I shouldn't. I want to be trustworthy and not take a chance on losing a friend's trust. Help me to be the kind of friend who always cares enough to be honest. That's the kind of friend I want, and the kind I want to be.

You keep the things that I tell You, God. And You lead me to tell my parents the things I shouldn't keep secret. Thank You, God, and good night.

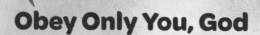

Obey Only You, God

[Satan] said to Jesus, "I will give You all
these nations if You will get down at my
feet and worship me." Jesus said to the
devil, "Get away, Satan. It is written,
'You must worship the Lord your
God. You must obey Him only.'"

MATTHEW 4:9–10

Satan wants to be You, God. But he is nothing like You. You are love; he is hate. You are good; he is bad. You want what is best and good for me; he wants to see me sad and knocked down.

Satan even wanted Your Son, Jesus, to bow down to him. Jesus told Satan to get away. He told him that everyone should worship and obey only You, God. You are perfect love and perfectly good. You want what's best for everyone.

I'm glad Jesus showed me that I should tell Satan to go away. I don't want him interfering in my life. I want *only* You. Thank You, and good night.

How Do I Pray?

"Pray like this: 'Our Father in heaven, Your name is holy. May Your holy nation come. What You want done, may it be done on earth as it is in heaven. Give us the bread we need today. Forgive us our sins as we forgive those who sin against us. Do not let us be tempted, but keep us from sin. Your nation is holy. You have power and shining-greatness forever. Let it be so.'"

MATTHEW 6:9–13

Jesus, You knew prayer could be hard, and that's why You taught us how to pray.

First, I praise You, God. Second, I need to tell You the things I have done wrong. It helps me to say them out loud and to let You know that I'm sorry for doing them. Third, I thank You for all the good things You're doing in my life, even when I can't see them happening. And fourth, I need to pray for others. Then I end by telling You that it's in Jesus' name that I ask.

I want to always talk to You honestly from my heart. Thank You for the example Jesus gave. Good night, God.

A King Who Shook

"I make a law that all those under my rule are to fear and shake before the God of Daniel. For He is the living God and He lives forever. His nation will never be destroyed and His rule will last forever. He saves and brings men out of danger, and shows His great power in heaven and on earth. And He has saved Daniel from the power of the lions."

DANIEL 6:26–27

Lions are scary. Hungry lions are extra scary. Daniel was thrown into a den of hungry lions by King Darius because Daniel prayed to You every day, God. It was something that King Darius didn't want to do, but it was the law. He was terrified and didn't eat or sleep all night until he came to check on Daniel. Daniel had survived and was alive and well! That's because You shut the mouths of the hungry lions.

Fear of You, God, is a good thing. Your enemies soon learn that. You are a good God who saves those who fear You and pray to You. Thank You, God. Good night.

Something New

A God-like life gives us much when we are happy for what we have. We came into this world with nothing. For sure, when we die, we will take nothing with us. If we have food and clothing, let us be happy.

1 TIMOTHY 6:6–8

I usually want to keep things the way I like them. I have food that I like, shows that I like to watch, music I listen to, and favorite clothes that I choose to wear. There's not always a lot of room to try anything new.

It's easy to get into the habit of doing things the same way. When someone has fixed a meal for me or wants me to watch something with them or has a new outfit they want me to try on, maybe I should try to do what they ask. I might even find something new that I like even better than the old.

Help me to be considerate and to be willing to try something new—especially if someone has gone to a lot of trouble for me or has something they want to share. Thanks, and good night, God.

Mean Girls

Open your mouth for those who cannot speak, and for the rights of those who are left without help.

PROVERBS 31:8

Sometimes girls can be mean, God. They pick on others and make them feel really bad about themselves. I think it's because sometimes mean girls can be unsure about themselves too. I don't want to be a mean girl. I want to stand up for the one who is being picked on. I want to let girls know that what's being said or done is wrong and that I don't want to have any part of it.

Speaking up can be scary. So can telling someone older what's happening. You stand up for people who are being picked on, God. You sent Your Son, Jesus, to let us know that You love us. And that You are there for us when we get picked on.

Thank You, God, that You show me that picking on someone is wrong. I don't ever want to be the one who's hurting someone. Good night, God.

Canceled

"Then the king took pity on his servant and let him go. He told him he did not have to pay the money back."
MATTHEW 18:27

When something gets canceled, it goes away. No one thinks of it anymore. Jesus told a story about a man who owed a lot of money to a king. If he couldn't pay the king, then he would go to jail. The king felt sorry for the man and had pity on him. The king canceled all the debt the man owed him. The man was free and didn't have to go to jail.

God cancels things too. He cancels sin. Payment for our sin is a huge debt that we *all* owe. Sin can overtake us, rule over us, and make us sick and miserable. But You cancel all my sins through Jesus. When I put my trust in Jesus, You forget all my past, present, and future sins.

Thank You, God, for having pity on me, for canceling my sin debt and forgiving what I owe. Good night, God.

Living in the Dark

Then God made the two great lights,
the brighter light to rule the day,
and the smaller light to rule the
night. He made the stars also.

GENESIS 1:16

I wouldn't want to live in complete darkness. You didn't want me to either, God. That's why You created the light, so there could be morning and evening. And that was just the first day of creation. You made daytime, which is the greater light. And You made the lesser light, the moon, to rule over the night so we would never be in complete darkness.

The sun that You made shines in the daytime and helps everything to grow. We couldn't survive without it. The evening light helps me to wind down and rest. You made the earth to spin around the sun, just as our lives should spin around Your Son.

Thank You that You shine Your daylight to brighten my way and for evening that helps me to rest. And thank You for the spinning earth that we live on. And mostly, that my life can spin around You. Good night, God.

Princess

"There are many rooms in My Father's house.
If it were not so, I would have told you.
I am going away to make a place for you."
JOHN 14:2

I like castles, God. They are big and beautiful. Mansions are big and beautiful too, like castles. There are many rooms in a mansion. Lots of people can live there together. That's how heaven will be, like one big, happy family.

Royalty, like princes and princesses, live in castles. Believers will be royalty in Your kingdom. You say that Your people will receive victors' crowns for living lives of faith in You. So I pray that I will always trust You and obey You, God, so that I will be an overcomer in this world and receive a reward from You.

Thank You for Your mansion with many rooms that You are getting ready for those who love You. Help me to always remember what I am working for—to be pleasing to You, God. Good night.

Wrong Way

He who listens to teaching is on the
path of life, but he who will not listen
to strong words goes the wrong way.

PROVERBS 10:17

Roads can take people in all different directions. If I'm going on a trip, I need to take the right road to get there. If I don't, I'll *never* get there. That works for how I live my life too. If I go down the wrong road, it will take me someplace I never wanted to go. That's why maps are important. They show the route.

God, You have maps and a route too. Your map is the Bible. There are sixty-six books in the Bible. You could call it Route 66 through the Bible. All the verses and the stories in it show me the route to take. It's the only way that leads to You, God. Any other way takes me away from You, and I would never want that.

I'm so happy to know that You gave me a map for Route 66. It has everything I need to have a safe and full trip through life with You, God. Good night.

Helping Out

Everyone of us will give an
answer to God about himself.
ROMANS 14:12

Sometimes I want to do grown-up things. Helping out around the house makes me feel good. Having responsibilities teaches me how to be dependable. I want others to be able to count on me. I also need to be responsible and dependable about sharing You, God. One day You will ask me what I've done with my life. I want to be able to tell You that I helped out the very best that I could.

I'm glad that others can count on me to help out wherever I'm needed. As I grow up, I want to do my share of work wherever I am. Thank You for the good feelings that follow when I'm responsible and dependable. Good night, God.

Two Are Better Than One

So comfort each other and make each other strong as you are already doing.
1 THESSALONIANS 5:11

Two or more people working together is always better than working alone. Two are better than one. One person by herself can be lonely, and work can be super hard. But having someone else helping to lift a heavy load makes a job a lot easier. Some loads are so heavy that the only way they can be moved is with the help of another.

That's how it is with people who are working through serious things too. When things are difficult, we need someone who will help us see every side, someone who will help us be strong and do the right thing. I want to be that someone who can help someone feel strong and better again.

I'm glad You will send me when people need help. Getting through hard times is easier when we have someone to lean on. Thank You for using me, God. Good night.

Ten Commandments

"But I show loving-kindness to thousands of those who love Me and keep My Laws."
EXODUS 20:6

God, You called Moses to go to the top of Mount Sinai. There You gave him a list of rules that everyone must follow. Moses was up there with You for forty days and forty nights. It was there that You carved into tablets of stone the rules called the Ten Commandments.

Those rules tell us to have no other gods beside You and to honor Your name and not misuse it in silly ways. It also tells us to keep the Sabbath holy, honor our fathers and mothers, and not to murder, cheat, steal, lie, or be jealous. These are good rules to live by that make everyone's lives better.

Thank You, God, for rules that never change. Help me to keep each one. Good night, God.

Calm the Storm

The followers came to awake Jesus.
They said, "Teacher! Teacher! We are
going to die!" Then Jesus got up and
spoke sharp words to the wind and the
high waves. The wind stopped blowing
and there were no more waves.

LUKE 8:24

Storms can be very scary. Being on a boat in a storm in the middle of the sea would be super scary. Tall waves tossing the boat could cause the boat to flip over or even sink. Jesus and His disciples were caught in a storm at sea, God. Jesus was asleep in their fishing boat when a storm blew in. The disciples were terrified and woke Jesus up. He spoke sharply to the wind and the waves, and they immediately stopped. That must have been something to see!

The wind and the waves can cause all kinds of damage, but they obey You, God. And if nature obeys You, then I don't have to fear anything, because that shows that You are in charge of everything!

I feel safe knowing that You control even the weather. You are awesome, God. Good night.

Meeting Up

"For all time to come this burnt gift is to be given at the door of the meeting tent before the Lord. There I will meet with you and speak to you."

EXODUS 29:42

My conversations with You are very important, God. When I talk to You, I need to find a quiet place so that I can think about what I'm saying to You. Things can get noisy, so I need to look for a place where I can be by myself.

You gave Your people a special place to meet with You and talk to You. It was called the Tent of Meeting because You met with them there. It was a holy and special place because of Your presence.

Help me to find a special place to meet with You, God. I'm glad You are never too busy or too tired to meet with me. Just like You're meeting with me right now. Thank You, God, and good night.

Many Languages

"Come, let Us go down and mix up their language so they will not understand what each other says." So the Lord sent them everywhere over the whole earth. And they stopped building the city.

GENESIS 11:7–8

In the beginning there was only one language, God. When You saw that mankind was trying to make a name for themselves and build a tower to heaven, You scattered them over the earth to build cities and populate the world.

By giving the people a lot of languages, You made it so they couldn't understand each other. When they realized they couldn't understand each other, they split up and went their own ways. That's how we came to have all the different cultures and people of all nations and languages.

Thank You for all the different cultures and people of the world, God. All the many differences make it much more interesting. Good night, God.

Accept Help

Help each other in troubles
and problems. This is the kind
of law Christ asks us to obey.
GALATIANS 6:2

Sometimes I like to do things on my own instead of asking for help. And there are times when I know that I'm doing something wrong, but I'm afraid or too shy to ask for help. There are some things that I can't do on my own and times when I should say, "I need help."

You want us to accept help from others when we need it. You put a lot of people on the earth so that people wouldn't be alone. Everyone has problems and needs help at one time or another. We shouldn't be embarrassed to reach out to someone.

Help me learn to reach out to others and not be afraid or too shy to ask for help. And help me to be there for anyone else who asks for help. Thank You, and good night, God.

Don't Dread

He will not be afraid of bad news. His heart
is strong because he trusts in the Lord.

PSALM 112:7

God, sometimes I dread things—like something I
don't know how to do, hearing bad news, or being
unprepared to do something. Dreading something
leaves a bad feeling in the pit of my stomach.

When I get this feeling, God, I know I need to talk
to someone about it. My parents are always there to
listen and help me figure out what to do to get rid
of the bad feelings. They might be able to explain
something to me or help me get ready for the thing
I'm dreading.

Thank You, God, for putting people in my life who
can help me figure out why I'm dreading something.
And thank You when the bad feeling in the pit of my
stomach leaves. Good night.

Found

"For God so loved the world that He gave His only Son. Whoever puts his trust in God's Son will not be lost but will have life that lasts forever."

JOHN 3:16

Sin separates me from You, God. It keeps me from having a forever, saving relationship with You. But You gave me a way back to You, God. That way is through Your only Son, Jesus Christ. He's the *only* way.

First, I need to tell You that I have sinned. And even the smallest bad thing I've done is still a sin. Then I need to ask You to forgive all my sins—past, present, and future. Next, I acknowledge that Jesus died on the cross for my sins and rose from the grave. Finally, I tell You with all my heart that I want to follow Jesus.

I pray for people everywhere that if they don't understand how to be saved, they will find a believer who can help them come to know You. Thank You for sending Your Son to save me and others, God. I'm thankful that You came to find me and I'm not lost and alone without You. Good night.

Hello! Are You Listening?

"Pharaoh will not listen to you. Then I will lay My hand on Egypt. By great acts that will punish the Egyptians, I will bring out My family groups, My people, the sons of Israel, from the land of Egypt. The Egyptians will know that I am the Lord when I put My hand upon Egypt and bring out the people of Israel from among them."

EXODUS 7:4–5

Sometimes it takes a lot to get my attention, God. Even if I'm warned, sometimes I just don't listen to what I'm told to do. That's what happened in Egypt.

You told Moses to tell Pharaoh, "Let my people go!" But Pharaoh didn't listen. In fact, he hardened his heart and continued to hurt Your people. So You sent ten plagues to get Pharaoh's attention. The stubborn pharaoh finally let Your people go.

God, I don't want You to have to go to great lengths to get my attention. I want to be ready to listen and obey whatever You tell me to do. Thank You for gentle warnings. Good night, God.

Tough Girl

Now Lappidoth's wife Deborah, a woman
who spoke for God, was judging Israel
at that time. She would sit under the
tree of Deborah between Ramah and
Bethel in the hill country of Ephraim.
And the people of Israel came to her
to find out what was right or wrong.
JUDGES 4:4–5

Deborah was a leader of Israel. Even though girls
didn't usually lead armies back then, You knew she
was able and strong enough to command an army.
She was very brave. She knew that You would go
ahead of her and bless all that she did. Deborah put
all her trust in You, knowing that the battle would
be won in Your might, not hers.

Knowing that You used a girl to do great and
courageous things helps me see that You can use
me too. I just need to do like Deborah did, to look to
You to go ahead of me and lead.

Thank You for brave girls who serve You, God.
Help me to be brave no matter what You ask me to
do. Good night, God.

Wise Guys

When they saw the star, they were filled
with much joy. They went into the house
and found the young Child with Mary,
His mother. Then they got down before
Him and worshiped Him. They opened
their bags of riches and gave Him gifts
of gold and perfume and spices.

MATTHEW 2:10–11

Magi were wise men who studied the stars. Even
kings would ask them to explain hard questions. They
saw the star in the east and followed it until they got
to the manger where the baby Jesus lay. When they
got to where Jesus was, they bowed down and said
they had come to worship the "King of the Jews."
They brought riches and gifts of gold, perfume, and
spices from afar. These wise guys were wise enough
to follow Your star and know that Jesus is King.

I want to be wise like the magi who were looking
for Jesus. And to bow down daily and worship Jesus.
I know that Jesus is King!

Thank You for the beautiful story of the star in
the east that pointed to where Jesus was. And thank
You for the things in my life that point to Jesus. Good
night, God.

Beautiful Feet

But how can they call on Him if they have not put their trust in Him? And how can they put their trust in Him if they have not heard of Him? And how can they hear of Him unless someone tells them? And how can someone tell them if he is not sent? The Holy Writings say, "The feet of those who bring the Good News are beautiful."

ROMANS 10:14–15

If I had some good news to tell but just kept it all to myself, that would be selfish. But the really good news is that Jesus died for the sins of all. And whoever believes in Jesus will be saved. It's not just good news, it's the best news!

God, You say that the feet of those who take the good news to others are beautiful. My feet are small, but they can carry Your love to those around me. I don't want to leave out anyone I know.

The good news is not heavy and doesn't take up any room because I carry it around in my heart on beautiful feet. Thank You, and good night, God.

Sister!

Martha was working hard getting the supper ready. She came to Jesus and said, "Do You see that my sister is not helping me? Tell her to help me." Jesus said to her, "Martha, Martha, you are worried and troubled about many things. Only a few things are important, even just one. Mary has chosen the good thing. It will not be taken away from her."

LUKE 10:40–42

Some sisters are alike, and some are very different, God. One might like to play house, while the other likes to play ball. And that's okay. Sisters don't have to be just alike. Martha and Mary were very different. Jesus came to visit the sisters and preach in their home. Martha was busy fixing meals for everyone, but she wasn't happy. She was so upset that she told on her sister.

But Jesus knew that it's important to feed our heads and hearts as well as our stomachs. It pleased Jesus that Mary wanted to learn from Him more than anything else.

I want to sit, listen, and learn about You, God. Thank You, and good night.

God Heard

The Lord made it possible for her to have a child, and when the time came she gave birth to a son. She gave him the name Samuel, saying, "I have asked the Lord for him."

1 SAMUEL 1:20

The name Samuel means "God has heard." Samuel's mother, Hannah, wanted a child very badly but couldn't have one until You heard her cries, God. Hannah promised You that if she had a son, she would dedicate his life to You. So when he was a young boy, she took him to the temple, to Eli the priest, to learn everything he could about You.

Hannah was very proud to watch her son grow tall and be used by You. Samuel became a judge over all of Israel and taught the importance of obedience to Your Word. It must have been very hard for Hannah to leave her son. But because You heard her, her son was used mightily to help Hannah and her people.

Thank You for hearing me when I call to You, God. Help me to never feel alone, because I know You will hear me. Good night.

A Special Daughter

But Ruth said, "Do not beg me to leave you or turn away from following you. I will go where you go. I will live where you live. Your people will be my people. And your God will be my God."

RUTH 1:16

Ruth and Naomi had a very special relationship, God. Ruth was Naomi's daughter-in-law. Ruth loved Naomi so much that after Ruth's husband, who was also Naomi's son, died, Ruth chose to be with her mother-in-law instead of going back home to her parents. Ruth hadn't grown up learning about You, God. But she loved Naomi so much that she said, "Your God will be my God."

God, it's good to have people in my life who are special. And it's good to be loyal to those I love. Daughters are special, but Ruth was very special. She was Naomi's whole life.

Thank You for special relationships, God, and for special daughters and moms, no matter how they come together. Good night.

Think about It

One of them turned back
when he saw he was healed. He
thanked God with a loud voice.
LUKE 17:15

While Jesus was on His way to a village, He came across ten men with a serious disease. They said, "Master, have pity on us." Jesus told them to go into town and show themselves to the priest. And as they were going, Jesus healed them. Only one man came back to Jesus and fell at His feet to thank Him. All ten had been healed, but only one was grateful enough to come back and show Jesus how thankful he was.

It's easy to take what You do for granted, God. We forget how big even the smallest things that You do for us are. I don't ever want to take You for granted. I always want to remember who helped me. And that's You, God.

Thank You for Your miracles and for Your healing. Good night, God.

Small People

Zaccheus wanted to see Jesus but he could not because so many people were there and he was a short man. He ran ahead and got up into a sycamore tree to see Him. Jesus was going by that way. When Jesus came to the place, He looked up and saw Zaccheus. He said, "Zaccheus, come down at once. I must stay in your house today."

LUKE 19:3–5

Zaccheus was a small man who wasn't very well liked. He was a dishonest tax collector who didn't get invited to people's houses very often. But that didn't keep wee little Zaccheus from wanting to see Jesus when He came to town. So up a sycamore tree he climbed. Jesus saw Zaccheus and told him He was going to come to his house that very day.

Being seen and heard can be difficult for a small person. But You, God, see everyone, even tiny little people who aren't very well liked. And Zaccheus's whole life was changed, all because Jesus took the time to let him know that he was loved.

Thank You that You take time for everyone, even the unlovable. Good night, God.

Priceless

Mary took a jar of special perfume
that cost much money and poured it
on the feet of Jesus. She dried His feet
with her hair. The house was filled with
the smell of the special perfume.

JOHN 12:3

When a person lives in a desert and all they have to wear on their feet are sandals, their feet get pretty dirty. Mary broke the jar of expensive perfume, everything she had, to have the honor of washing Jesus' feet. She then dried His feet with her long hair. Mary knew that Jesus was worth everything she had.

I want to be like Mary. I want to be willing to give Jesus everything I have. She knew she was cleaning the feet of God. And that was priceless.

Thank You for Mary who got to show Jesus how much she loved Him. Help me find ways to show my love to You too. Good night, God.

Clean Feet

"I am your Teacher and Lord. I have washed your feet. You should wash each other's feet also. I have done this to show you what should be done. You should do as I have done to you."

JOHN 13:14–15

Jesus washed the feet of His disciples to show us how we are to serve others. Even though He is King, Jesus lowered Himself to wash people's dirty feet, something only a servant would ordinarily do. He wanted us to see that life is not about what others can do for us but about what we can do for others. And no one is ever too big or too important to take care of another's needs.

But Jesus didn't just clean their feet, He cleaned their hearts. He cleans our hearts by forgiving our sins.

God, help me never to feel like I'm too important to do nice things for others. And help me to always remember that You are the One who cleans feet and hearts. Thank You, and good night, God.

Remember

When He had given thanks, He broke it
and said, "Take this bread and eat it. This
is My body which is broken for you. Do this
to remember Me." In the same way after
supper, He took the cup. He said, "This cup
is the New Way of Worship made between
God and you by My blood. Whenever
you drink it, do it to remember Me."

1 CORINTHIANS 11:24–25

On Jesus' last evening on earth, He sat down and had
His last supper with His disciples. He thanked You,
God, for the meal, then gave the disciples bread and
wine. He did that so they would remember all He had
done for them.

We should remember the special things and
people in our lives. And Jesus is the most special
and most important person ever to walk on earth.

Mealtime is a good time to remember, talk about,
and be thankful for all the good things that happened
during the day and everything that Jesus has done
for us. Thank You, God, for Jesus. Help me always to
remember all that He did for me. Good night.

Coming Back

They said, "You men of the country of
Galilee, why do you stand looking up into
heaven? This same Jesus Who was taken
from you into heaven will return in the
same way you saw Him go up into heaven."
ACTS 1:11

When Jesus had finished everything He came to do on earth, He was taken up into a cloud and couldn't be seen anymore. Two men dressed in white told those still looking up that Jesus was in heaven but would return one day. They said that He would come back just as He had left. One day Jesus will come back for all those who love Him. It will be an awesome day.

I'm glad that Jesus is with You, God. And that both of You are looking down at me. I feel safe and loved, knowing that one day Jesus will come back for me.

I want to be like Jesus so that You will say that I have done well, God. Knowing Jesus is the best thing that ever happened to me, and I want to be ready when He comes back. Thank You, and good night, God.